The Economics of Empire

The Économics
of Empire:

Britain, Africa and the New Imperialism 1870-95

William G. Hynes

Longman Group Limited London

Associated companies, branches and
representatives throughout the world

© Longman Group Ltd 1979

First published 1979

ISBN 0 582 64234 5 (cased)
         64235 3 (paper)

Printed in Great Britain by
Western Printing Services Ltd, Bristol

Contents

Preface ix
1 Introduction: economics and Empire; the nature of the problem 1
2 The early 1870s: the free-traders' indifference towards Empire 13
3 Economic recession and the first signs of a new commercial imperialism 22
4 The business slump of the mid 1880s: transition to the imperialism of free trade 40
5 The imperialism of free trade: Africa in the mid 1880s 57
6 International competition and imperial expansion in the late 1880s 88
7 The recession of the early 1890s: the climax of commercial imperialism 109
8 Conclusion: business recession and imperial expansion 134
Select Bibliography 143
Index 155

List of Maps

South-east Asia   152
Tropical Africa (east and west)   153
Southern Africa   154

Abbreviations

AMGC	*Annual Meeting of the Glasgow Chamber of Commerce*
CC	Chamber of Commerce
CCJ	*Chamber of Commerce Journal*
CO	Colonial Office
EcHR	*Economic History Review*
Econ	*The Economist*
FO	Foreign Office
GFAC	*Minutes of the Foreign Affairs Committee of the Glasgow Chamber of Commerce*
JAH	*Journal of African History*
LCCR	*Report of the London Chamber of Commerce*
LDC	*Liverpool Daily Courier*
LEIC	*Minutes of the East India and China Committee of the Liverpool Chamber of Commerce*
LJC	*Liverpool Journal of Commerce*
LSAS	*Minutes of the South African Section of the London Chamber of Commerce*
LWAS	*Minutes of the West African Section of the London Chamber of Commerce*
MASEC	*Minutes of the African Sectional Committee of the Manchester Chamber of Commerce*
MBCC	*Minutes of the Council of the Birmingham Chamber of Commerce*
MG	*Manchester Guardian*
MGCC	*Minutes of the Board of Directors of the Glasgow Chamber of Commerce*
MLCC	*Minutes of the Council of the Liverpool Chamber of Commerce*

MP	*Mackinnon Papers*
PCCE	*Report of the Proceedings of the Congress of Chambers of Commerce of the Empire*
PMCC	*Proceedings of the Manchester Chamber of Commerce*
PP	*Parliamentary Papers*
RACC	*Report of the Association of Chambers of Commerce of the United Kingdom*
RBCC	*Report of the Birmingham Chamber of Commerce*
RCDT	Royal Commission on the Depression of Trade and Industry
RGCC	*Report of the Glasgow Chamber of Commerce*
RLCC	*Report of the Liverpool Chamber of Commerce*

Preface

There has been much debate in recent years over the nature of economic imperialism. While the end of the nineteenth century is commonly seen as the great age of imperialism, there is still intense controversy over the role of economics in the main imperialist exercise of the period, the partition of tropical Africa. Interpretations of imperialism as an outgrowth of European finance capitalism, perhaps relevant to South Africa, are not easily applicable to tropical Africa where European investment was virtually nonexistent until very recently. This, however, does not rule out the importance of economic motives in the partition of tropical Africa. As this book will attempt to demonstrate, there was indeed a consistent pattern of economic motivation behind late Victorian expansionism and the partition of tropical Africa was decisively influenced by a series of sharp crises in the British economy between 1870 and 1895.

For their help in locating the material upon which this book is based I wish to record my thanks to the officers and staff of the British Museum, the Public Record Office, the Institute of Historical Research of London, the Liverpool Public Library, the Manchester Public Library and Dalhousie University's Killam Library. I wish also to thank the Secretaries of the Birmingham, Glasgow and London Chambers of Commerce and the firm of John Holt and Company of Liverpool. This study evolved out of a Ph.D. thesis submitted to Dalhousie University. I am grateful to the Canada Council for financial support during my research in the United Kingdom. I am particularly indebted to Professor John E. Flint of Dalhousie University who supervised my doctoral dissertation and provided tremendous assistance at every stage in the preparation of this book. Professor H. C. Mui of Memorial University read the entire manuscript and made a number of helpful suggestions. My greatest debt of gratitude, however, is to my wife who assisted in my research and provided constant help and encouragement throughout the preparation of this study.

One

Introduction: economics and Empire; the nature of the problem

Imperialism is one of the most emotive issues of our time. Vaguely used to describe the overt or veiled domination of one group, country or nation by another, the word 'imperialism' has acquired a universal opprobrium. The late nineteenth century is commonly thought of as the 'age of imperialism', a period when Europeans and people of European descent extended their domination to embrace directly or indirectly almost the whole of the non-European world. Though this imperialist control has almost everywhere been broken, its repercussions continue to have world-wide significance. Third World leaders denounce the 'neo-imperialism' of the West and the Soviet Union. At the same time, some of the bitterest foes of empire have themselves fallen into a kind of sub-imperialism, grasping for regional mastery within areas of the world under the indirect hegemony of one of the present-day 'super-powers'.

What is the motivation behind imperialism and what are its historical origins? Imperialism is no recent development. In a sense, the 'age of imperialism' was itself the outcome of a long process that began when Christopher Columbus set sail for America in the fifteenth century. But imperialism existed before Columbus's day; evidence from historians and archaeologists suggests that empires rose and fell long before mankind learned to keep written records. There is, however, a profound difference between modern imperialism—if that term may be used to refer to the period since the nineteenth century—and earlier processes of empire building. Modern imperialism differs sharply from all similar developments in the past because it has its roots in the Industrial Revolution.

The Industrial Revolution was the most fundamental transformation of human life since the invention of agriculture. Britain was the first country in the world to industrialise and for a time in the nineteenth century she occupied the unique position of being the 'workshop of the world'. From the four quarters of the globe raw materials were shipped to British factories to be turned into manufactured goods, the bulk of which in turn was exported to markets overseas. Most of this vast import and export trade was carried in British ships. By the mid nineteenth century, huge amounts of capital flowed overseas as British investors and speculators opened up new continents and laid the foundations for industrialisation in other countries. Britain was the centre of a new global economy, the hub of a complex network of multilateral flows of goods and capital which was rapidly transforming the world.

Industrialisation brought fundamental social changes, the most significant and far-reaching of which was the emergence by the second half of the nineteenth century of a new class structure in Britain. A few of those who were able to accumulate wealth by taking advantage of the new opportunities of industrialisation were assimilated into the British aristocracy, which had traditionally replenished itself with fresh blood from outside its own ranks. But the majority came increasingly to recognise themselves as a separate group in society, a middle class. Their outlook was shaped by popularised maxims from utilitarian philosophy and *laissez faire* economics blended with the practical wisdom of the enterprising individual, hard work, thrift and strict personal morality. To accumulate and invest capital in profitable ventures and to buy cheap and sell dear were not only in the individual's best interest but also in the best interests of society in general. Few Victorians doubted that commerce and industry throve best when untouched by the dead hand of the state and that free trade among nations was part of the natural order of things. Armed with these convictions and the moral certitude that came with material success, the Victorian middle classes believed themselves to be on the right path to contentment in this world and salvation in the next.

Industrialisation also brought revolutionary changes in the role of labour. With the spread of the factory system, labour became increasingly the labour of proletarians, that is men who unlike their counterparts in pre-industrial societies have no source of income apart from their wages and whose sole link with their employer is a 'cash nexus'. Becoming rapidly urbanised, frequently under appalling living conditions, this group was numerically the most important in British society. Yet the growth of the British economy did not depend on the purchasing power of the working people. Economists, businessmen and politicans assumed that wages would not rise above the level required for subsistence. Because domestic mass consumption remained so low throughout most of the nineteenth century economic development required the continuous expansion of the perimeters of the new industrial system, bringing more and more of the world within its ever-widening orbit. The two chief preoccupations of Victorian businessmen were the rate of their profits and the rate of expansion of their markets. These concerns lay behind much of the dynamic expansionism of the nineteenth-century economy.

By the third quarter of the nineteenth century British manufacturers, traders, investors, shipowners and railway builders were expanding the frontiers of the economy on a global scale. From British Columbia to Argentina and from the Niger River to Hong Kong, businessmen exploited the advantages of Britain's industrial and commercial supremacy. For the most part this was a matter of private enterprise; officials were not directly involved, nor in the case of the tropics were colonists. Trade, not rule or settlement, was the primary objective in the populated regions of Africa and Asia. But where there were obstacles to free trade abroad, the aid of the state was sometimes invoked. In the mid-Victorian period, diplomacy, intimidation and naval blockade were used to persuade 'corrupt' Chinese mandarins or 'savage' African kings to open their dominions to peaceful free-traders. Sometimes even annexations were believed to be necessary, as for example in Lagos in 1861. These, however, were regarded as unfortunate exceptions. For most of the nineteenth century, the acquisition of tropical dependencies ran counter to the strongest prejudices of the most influential classes in Victorian society. Apart from their dislike of colonies in general, tropical regions held a very low priority in the estimation of the British business community for most of the nineteenth century.

The reasons for this are not hard to find. Though the network of British trade and investment was worldwide, it tended to be concentrated overwhelmingly in areas of the world that were relatively well developed. In the third quarter of the nineteenth century

Europe and North America were still Britain's chief partners in trade and investment, as they had been since the beginning of the century. The colonies of settlement came far behind Latin America in importance to the British economy. Of the tropical and semi-tropical world, only the Indian trade was of major significance. By and large, Africa and Asia were of peripheral value to the nineteenth-century British economy; they attracted little capital and absorbed only a small fraction of Britain's manufactures. Nor were the tropics crucial as suppliers of raw materials. Only once during the nineteenth century—at the time of the so-called cotton famine during the American Civil War—was there anything like a major crisis of supply in the industrialised world. If for some reason supplies were cut off from one region, they could easily be drawn from other equally accessible areas. No single tropical country or group of countries had exclusive control of a strategic industrial material and few in any case were capable of enforcing a monopoly.

For most of the nineteenth century the bias and preference of British businessmen reflected and reinforced the existing patterns of trade and investment. Businessmen assumed that Europe, the United States and to some extent Latin America would continue to be their chief partners in economic advance. Trade with Asia and Africa was of course encouraged where possible but for the first three-quarters of the nineteenth century there was no significant commercial pressure for the integration of these regions into the expanding international British economy.

Why then was so much of the undeveloped tropical world carved up by the British and other Europeans in the last quarter of the nineteenth century? The question is one that has perplexed historians for a long time. One of the earliest explanations was that originally put forward by the Englishman J. A. Hobson and subsequently modified by Lenin and others[1] into what may most conveniently be called the classic economic interpretation of imperialism. According to this theory, there was an inevitable tendency for the rate of profit to decline as the nineteenth-century European economies became fully industrialised. As investment became less profitable at home, increasingly large surpluses of capital were invested in undeveloped regions overseas where, because of the greater risks involved, returns were much higher. This process is held to have led inevitably to the takeover of undeveloped areas by industrialised countries, since the owners of capital manipulated national governments into extending imperial rule to protect their overseas investments.

It is not difficult to demonstrate—and it has been repeatedly pointed out by recent historians[2]—that most of these assumptions will not bear closer scrutiny in terms of British imperialism. For one thing, the bulk of British trade and investment was outside the Empire in the last quarter of the nineteenth century. Moreover, it has been shown that the returns on overseas investment were generally not significantly higher than those obtainable from certain classes of domestic investments. Furthermore, at least in the case of Britain, the different versions of the classic economic theory fail to provide convincing or verifiable explanations of the process whereby economic forces were translated into government policies. It is not enough simply to allude to the sinister machinations of capitalists; the methods which businessmen used to bring pressure on government must be demonstrated by historical evidence. This is something that has not been adequately done by the main proponents of the classic economic interpretation of imperialism.

The chief proponents of the classic economic interpretation were writing before the Second World War. Since 1945 a vast amount of historical material has become available on the expansion of Europe overseas in the late nineteenth century. This material is especially rich in the case of British expansion in Africa. As private and government documents on the partition period became available to historians and interest in the emergent nations of Africa stimulated research into their past, studies of imperialism began to shift their focus from the metropolis to the periphery of the Empire. Much recent historical writing seems to suggest that events on the frontiers provide the key to an understanding of imperial expansion. This kind of approach has been generalised into a broad interpretation of late Victorian imperialism by John Gallagher and Ronald Robinson in their *Africa and the Victorians: The Official Mind of Imperialism*.[3] For Robinson and Gallagher imperialism was no more than a reaction to changes on the frontiers of empire; expansion occurred as the result of British responses to new challenges abroad rather than because of events within the metropolitan society. The main challenge in the late nineteenth century was the increasing disruption of non-European societies under the pressures of Western influences in the form of missionaries, traders and travellers. Still, it was necessary to explain why British statesmen responded to

5

these challenges by establishing formal rule in many non-European parts of the world. For this purpose the authors of *Africa and the Victorians* developed the concept of a 'collective mind of government' or 'official mind'. This notion was based on the assumption that British foreign and colonial policy was made by a governing *élite* operating according to a set of principles peculiar to itself. Though this *élite* was not entirely immune to extraneous pressures from home or abroad, the primary determinants of its policies and actions were the prejudices, beliefs and traditions of the Victorian governing classes. So far as Africa was concerned, the preoccupation of these aristocratic officials with the security of the Cape and Suez routes to India was the main principle behind British imperialism in the late nineteenth century. Far from originating in deep-seated factors in the metropolitan economy, imperialism is seen as a kind of historical accident resulting from more or less fortuitous events on the frontier.

This interpretation is noteworthy because it is the first serious attempt to provide a general explanation of imperialism using the wealth of historical material that has become available since the Second World War. But its failure to provide an adequate account of imperialism in areas other than Africa is not the most damaging flaw in this theory. A far greater defect is Robinson's and Gallagher's attempt to gloss over completely the socio-economic aspects of imperialism by inventing the dubious concept of an 'official mind'. Imperialism appears as nothing more than the reluctant and bungling activity of a series of more or less benevolent aristocrats in Whitehall. The central fact about nineteenth-century imperialism, its origins in the industrial system, is entirely ignored. In this respect the classic economic interpretation is closer to the truth, though as outlined above it too is open to serious objections.

Despite the vast amount of discussion of imperialism and the widespread assumption by many of its present-day critics that their economic system forces the Western powers to seek continued domination of the Third World, our understanding of the economics of empire is still very unclear. To be sure, there are mountains of books on the subject. Many of them, however, contain highly theoretical arguments which often pay little attention to the world of concrete historical fact. There have been few efforts to explain the economic motivation behind modern imperialism using the wealth of historical material and specialised studies that have become available in the last few decades. [4] A number of recent scholars have attempted to relate their detailed accounts of events in various parts of the former British Empire to social and economic conditions in the metropolis, [5] but none has really succeeded in bridging the gap between a narration of the political and diplomatic events of traditional imperial history and a detailed analysis of developments in the metropolitan economy. [6] The present study attempts to fill this hiatus in our knowledge and break new methodological ground in its approach to imperial history.

There are two main problems that appear to confront any serious attempt to explore the relationship between imperial expansion and the problems of the late Victorian economy. In the first place, any explanation of late nineteenth-century imperialism must come to grips with the partition of Africa, since that was certainly the most dramatic and possibly the most important manifestation of Victorian expansionism. Here statistics of trade and investment and the other tools of the economic historian may be somewhat misleading. At no time during the partition did Africa absorb more than a tiny fraction of Britain's exports of goods or capital. However, it would be wrong to conclude from this alone that economic factors played no part in British motivation during the partition. Sometimes hopes and expectations were a more accurate measure of economic motivation than statistics of actual trade or investment. Those who searched for new markets in the late-nineteenth century were no less economically motivated because they sought in vain than those who in an earlier period sought the riches of India in the wilds of North America. In fact the very lack of accurate information about the economic potential of Africa and Asia in the late nineteenth century may have led to an exaggerated optimism about their actual economic value.

A second major problem in any attempt to understand the connections between economics and empire in late Victorian Britain arises from the highly technical and controversial nature of most recent studies of the late nineteenth-century economy. Throughout the whole of the nineteenth century British economic growth was punctuated by cyclical fluctuations or periodic ups and downs in the level of business activity. These fluctuations have been the cause of considerable interest in recent years but it is the sequence of boom and slump in the final quarter of the century that has attracted the greatest amount of attention among economic historians. This is largely because of the claim that these years constitute a watershed in British economic history, a period during which the industrialisation of other countries, the increase of competition in world trade and a slowing down in the rate of British industrial growth suggests the end of an era of British economic supremacy. More particularly, it is claimed that the years from 1873 to 1896 can be seen as a distinct economic period, that of the Great Depression of the nineteenth century.[7]

Suggestions that the appearance of imperialism at the time of the Great Depression was more than coincidental are by no means new, but little research has been done on the precise nature of the relationship, partly because of the complexity of the economic issues involved. However, even though the dust of controversy over the Great Depression has not yet settled, one thing at least is clear: whatever their nature and causes, the economic problems of the last quarter of the nineteenth century led to a serious decline in the confidence of British businessmen. The mid-Victorian beliefs in free trade and the self-adjusting interaction of supply and demand in the market place were badly shaken by the severity of the economic disturbances in the closing decades of the nineteenth century. This would suggest that whatever economic historians have said about the overall performance of the late Victorian economy, the views of contemporaries still have to be taken into account in any assessment of the effects of the economic forces at work. Businessmen, then as now, were deeply concerned with ups and downs in the economy and tended to base their calculations on their own perceptions of short-run conditions rather than on sophisticated analyses of long-term trends. Thus, a study of contemporary business reactions to short-term fluctuations in the economy may prove to be a fruitful line of inquiry into the relationship between economic recession and imperial expansion.

Business attitudes should provide an important link between economic forces, as measured by the indices of production, trade and profits on the one hand, and government policies in the imperial field on the other. If economic recession at home is relevant to an understanding of imperial expansion abroad, it would seem that business attitudes towards empire should reflect this relationship. This is not to say that business opinion would reflect only economic conditions in the short run; businessmen may also have been influenced by broader social and economic currents at the time. Nor would it be sufficient for our purposes merely to attempt to correlate changes in business attitudes towards empire with fluctuations in the level of economic activity. If there was a causal connection between recession and business desire for imperial expansion, the relationship must be clearly demonstrated. Likewise, if business pressures were responsible for imperial expansion, it is necessary that the linkages be explicitly shown. Since the formal separation of government and economy with the dismantling of the mercantilist system in the first half of the nineteenth century, the relationship between the two became much more complex. However, there can be no doubt that the political system was highly responsive to the requirements of trade and industry during the free-trade era. Throughout the whole of this period successive British governments accepted the responsibility of encouraging the growth of British overseas trade.[8] The general promotion of trade abroad was one of the main principles of British foreign policy and the interests of merchants and industrialists needed no special pleading at home. Nonetheless British businessmen would be constantly on the alert to make certain that the government was doing all it could to promote overseas trade, especially during bouts of recession at home.

In examining late Victorian business attitudes it is necessary to draw certain broad distinctions on methodological grounds. The business community can be broken down roughly into its major components of industry, trade and finance. While these distinctions were not always maintained in practice, industry and trade were generally free from the control of banking until at least 1900. Before the days of direct merchandising by large manufacturing firms, the wholesale merchant played an indispensable role in the distribution of goods and by and large remained a figure quite distinct from the industrialist. Although all parts of the business community were affected by cyclical recession, merchants were usually hit first and hardest by downturns in the business cycle. Merchants were also the group most directly concerned with market conditions at home and abroad. Accordingly, the present study will focus principally on mercantile attitudes, though industrial and financial opinion receive some consideration. Within this general framework it is necessary to examine the effects of recession on particular industries. Our analysis will lack precision unless we establish which groups were affected and how severely they suffered or thought themselves to be suffering from downturns in the economy.

Of particular British industries, cotton was in many ways the most important. The cotton industry was the leading sector of the British economy for the whole of the nineteenth century. Its importance to industrialisation in general and particularly its contribution to the process of capital formation would be hard to over-estimate. In an age when the majority of people, even in the most economically advanced countries, spent the bulk of their incomes on the basic necessities of food, clothing and shelter, world demand for its products was seemingly insatiable. By 1871 the output of no other British industry was worth so much as that of cotton manufacture. Even more important was the role of cotton in the international British economy; much of British shipping and overseas trade in general depended on the fortunes of the cotton industry. In examining mercantile responses to recession, particular attention will be paid to the cotton industry.

It will be obvious that completeness in such a survey of late nineteenth-century British mercantile opinion is practically unattainable. Even if every businessman who had definite views on the national economy committed his thoughts to paper, a comprehensive file of these opinions would be virtually impossible to compile. However, it is possible to obtain a fairly accurate cross section of mercantile opinion at any given point in time. Since businessmen concerned with influencing policy do not generally operate singly as individuals but in groups or associations, records of chambers of commerce and other mercantile pressure groups, commercial publications and information given by business groups in official inquiries and correspondence with government departments should provide sufficient material to construct a profile of business opinion on the state of the economy. This profile should tell us where and why commercial pressure was exerted in the sphere of foreign and colonial affairs. We can then examine these areas in more detail to discover how and with what effect mercantile pressure was brought to bear on the decision-making processes of government.

An analysis of the effects of economic forces on governmental decisions is complicated by the fact that economic changes occurred in a more desultory fashion and over relatively longer periods of time than the processes of political decision making. Current deterministic models and conspiracy theories fail to do justice to the complexities of the relationship between economic impulse and political decision. Our method will be more empirical. Records of the Foreign and Colonial Offices are used together with specialised secondary studies to assess the impact of commercial pressures on government decisions to advance or maintain the frontiers of the Empire.

We shall be concerned with such diverse parts of the former British Empire as Canada and Burma but the chief focus of our attention will be tropical Africa, the main arena for European expansion in the late nineteenth century. It should be stressed, however, that the present study is not an attempt to write a history of the partition of Africa, let alone a history of the British Empire in the late nineteenth century. Nor does it purport to analyse the late Victorian economy to prove or disprove the existence of the Great Depression from 1873 to 1896. Rather it is an attempt to understand the relationship between two major historical themes, the economic recessions of the last quarter of the nineteenth century and late Victorian overseas expansion. This is not to imply that the nature of imperialism can be comprehended entirely within the framework of the present short study. If relatively little is said about southern Africa, India or the colonies of European settlement, it is not because these areas are unimportant to an understanding of imperialism but because there were other pressures acting for colonial expansion of a different sort from that which took place in tropical Africa. A full treatment of the economic motivation of imperialism would have to include, for example, a detailed study of the pressures exerted by London financial interests. However, by examining some of the connections between business recessions in Britain and British imperialism in tropical Africa in the late nineteenth century we hope to unravel a few of the intricacies in the economics of empire.

Notes

[1] See, for examples, V. I. Lenin, *Imperialism: the Highest Stage of Capitalism*, New York, 1934 ed.; Rosa Luxemburg, *The Accumulation of Capital*, trans. by Agnes Schwarzschild, New York, 1968; Parker T. Moon, *Imperialism and World Politics*, New York, 1944.

² See, for examples, D. K. Fieldhouse, 'Imperialism: An Historiographical Revision', *Economic History Review*, 2nd ser., xiv, 1961, pp. 187–209; D. S. Landes, 'Some Thoughts on the Nature of Economic Imperialism', *Journal of Economic History*, xxi, 1961, pp. 496–512; R. J. Hammond, 'Imperialism: Sidelights on a Stereotype', *Journal of Economic History*, xxi, 1961, pp. 582–98.

³ London, 1961.

⁴ A notable exception is D. K. Fieldhouse, *Economics and Empire*, London, 1973.

⁵ See, for example, G. N. Uzoigwe, *Britain and the Conquest of Africa*, Ann Arbor, Mich., 1974.

⁶ At least not in English. For a brilliant socio-economic analysis of German imperialism in the late nineteenth century, see Hans-Ulrich Wehler, *Bismarck und der Imperialismus*, Cologne, 1972.

⁷ Two excellent guides to the voluminous literature on this subject are S. B. Saul, *The Myth of the Great Depression*, London, 1969; and D. H. Aldcroft and H. W. Richardson, *The British Economy 1870–1939*, London, 1969.

⁸ See D. C. M. Platt, *Finance, Trade and Politics in British Foreign Policy 1815–1914*, Oxford, 1968.

Two

The early 1870s: the free-traders' indifference towards Empire

The boom in business activity in the early seventies reached its peak in 1873. Although movements in prices, production, foreign trade and employment did not all follow precisely the same course in these years, the general pattern was unmistakable: most industries and trades recorded unprecedented levels of activity. Between 1870 and 1873 British gross domestic product rose by 22 per cent. The value of exports rose even faster, increasing by 26 per cent between 1870 and 1872.[1] Prosperity was reflected in and reinforced by the confident mood in commercial circles.[2] Businessmen were highly optimistic about the future of the economy and they felt an ebullient pride in the accomplishments of their free-trading economic system. Free trade was widely regarded as the wellspring of the country's prosperity and the key to continuous economic progress. It was the cornerstone of an economic system that appeared to possess the admirable quality of being entirely self-regulating; the forces of supply and demand being continually adjusted by the 'natural' mechanism of the market-place.

Since the conclusion of the Anglo-French commercial treaty of 1860—the so-called Cobden Treaty—British merchants and manufacturers hoped that free trade would eventually become the universal pattern of inter-European commerce. With the French example before them, other continental nations were expected to adopt free trade, the net result of which would be a great increase in Britain's trade with her European neighbours. These sanguine expectations were encouraged during the 1860s when slightly under 40 per cent of Britain's total exports went to the Continent.[3] By 1870, when it came up for renewal, the Cobden Treaty was regarded as backward by many ardent free-traders, who considered that complete free trade between Britain and France was long over-due. British businessmen urged their government to use the occasion of the treaty negotiations to bring about a further liberalisation of Anglo-French trade. It was widely believed in British business circles that despite the protectionist tendencies of certain leading French politicians, the majority of Frenchmen were free-traders at heart.[4]

But France was exhausted after her struggle with Prussia and the French Government, seeking increased revenue, proposed to levy higher taxes on imported raw materials and manufactures. However, this proposal was still-born, for the French National Assembly refused to accept duties on raw materials. In 1873, the Cobden Treaty was extended until 1877,[5] a step which appeared to confirm the British conviction that protectionism in France was a spent force.

This belief in the inevitability of free trade with Europe had important consequences for British business attitudes towards areas of the world like Africa and Asia. So long as businessmen believed that the greatest growth in the market for British exports would occur in areas that were already good customers, there was no great pressure to open new markets elsewhere. Despite some differences between colonial and metropolitan tariffs, metropolitan policy was generally followed in French overseas territory and liberal trade conditions obtained in most French colonial possessions.[6] Since French colonies thus provided increased scope for British overseas trade, British merchants saw no reason to oppose French activity in Africa or Asia.

Business attitudes towards the colonies of settlement in these years were characterised chiefly by indifference, mixed with a feeling of irritation against colonial import duties, particularly those of Canada. An increase in the Canadian tariff in the late 1860s led to a fall of some 20 per cent in British exports to that country and provoked much resentment in commercial circles in Britain. The Birmingham Chamber of Commerce felt that the 15 per cent duty imposed by Canada on British manufactures was especially unfair in view of the expenditures by the British Government on the defence of the Colony.[7] The Association of Chambers of Commerce of the United Kingdom urged the British Government to make the strongest possible representations to all the colonies to adopt the principle of tariffs for revenue purposes only. The Association claimed that protective tariffs were not only contrary to the canons of free trade but also that they were against the true self-interest of the colonies, since they tended to create manufacturing industries for which the colonies were unsuited.[8] The directors of the Manchester Chamber of Commerce complained that Britain was supporting the imperial army and navy chiefly for the benefit of the colonies and they urged the Secretary of State for Colonial Affairs to make every effort to persuade colonial governments to reduce their duties on British manufactured goods.[9]

Despite their complaints about colonial tariffs, few British businessmen would have gone so far as to suggest that colonial separation would be in the best interests of the mother country. Some pointed out that if Canada were not part of the Empire, her duties on British goods would probably be even higher. Others felt that although the British economy was in an extremely prosperous state, the colonies were a kind of insurance against any future threat to Britain's industrial and commercial supremacy. As R. A. Macfie, M.P., told an audience of Liverpool businessmen in May 1872: 'a variety of circumstances might deprive England of that start in the race of manufacture on which she had so long thriven, and we should be prepared, by means of outlets in the colonies, for the day when England's pre-eminence might pass away and employment was needed for the people'.[10] F. Prange, President of the Liverpool Chamber of Commerce, agreed with Macfie; he suggested that Liverpool should take steps 'to direct public attention more emphatically to the utilisation of the British colonies'.[11] However, it was to take another decade before such sentiments became sufficiently widespread among businessmen to lead to serious attempts further to cement the imperial connection between the mother country and the colonies of settlement.

India attracted more attention than the settlement colonies in the early 1870s. This was particularly true in Manchester, for the cotton famine of the previous decade was still fresh in the minds of Manchester businessmen. With the production of cotton manufactures at an unprecedented level, they looked to India as a potential major supplier of raw cotton should the American supply again be interrupted. It was as a supplier of an essential raw material rather than as a major consumer of manufactures that the Manchester merchants most valued India until the late 1870s. But few businessmen believed that the fortunes of the cotton industry were entirely bound up with the fate of India. In the early 1870s there was even some speculation in commercial circles about future self government in India.[12]

If there was little interest in business circles in the Empire as it stood in the early 1870s, there was even less desire to expand it in faraway places like Africa and Asia. British merchants in these areas frequently sought the support of commercial opinion in the metropolis to back their demands for government intervention in their diverse spheres of interest. For most of the 1870s, however, businessmen in Britain turned a deaf ear to pleas for intervention in distant non-colonial regions. With a business boom at home and a buoyant demand for British goods in the 'civilised' markets of the world in these years, areas of low consuming power like Africa and the Far East held few attractions for British trade and industry.

For almost half a century after the signing of the Treaty of Tientsin in June 1858 Anglo-Chinese commercial and diplomatic relations revolved around the interpretation of that document. Throughout this whole period the demands of merchants in the China trade embodied essentially the same aims: the opening of more and more of China to European trade. This, in the merchants' opinion, meant chiefly the increased use of British pressure to force the Chinese to adhere to existing treaty engagements and to remove restrictions on the movement of traders and goods in the interior of China. But British authorities took a different view of Anglo-Chinese relations. During the 1860s the official British policy towards China was one of supporting the Chinese central government while encouraging gradual internal reforms; the British Government refused to play a direct role in opening up China to foreign trade.[13] Thus there was a fundamental cleavage between the attitudes of British officials and the China merchants in these years. The latter were well organised in chambers of commerce in the treaty ports and in the powerful Committee of London Merchants which represented the major British commercial interests in China. But despite intensive lobbying in British business circles, they were unable to win support for their proposals for direct British pressure to force radical fiscal and administrative changes upon the Chinese provinces. There was clearly no desire in British commercial circles for intervention in the internal affairs of China.[14]

While some China merchants believed that the commercial

penetration of the 'Celestial Kingdom' could be accomplished by greatly extending the treaty port system, others argued that China could be more easily opened to British trade by the establishment of direct communications between British possessions in Burma and the Chinese interior. Since the late 1850s when Captain Richard Sprye, a retired Indian Army officer, had attempted to interest British commercial opinion in opening a route from Rangoon to Yunnan, some merchants believed that the four hundred million potential buyers of Halifax woollens, Manchester cottons and Sheffield hardware could be more easily reached via an overland route from British possessions in Burma than through the Chinese treaty ports. At the instigation of Lord Cranbourne, the Secretary of State for India in 1866, the Indian Government undertook to survey two routes, including the one proposed by Captain Sprye, between Burma and western China. However, the survey of the Sprye route was only half completed when Sir Stafford Northcote, Cranbourne's successor at the India Office, dropped the project.[15] Business circles in Britain had shown no great enthusiasm for the scheme and there was no commercial pressure for its revival at the time.

Although British merchants expressed their general approval of plans for the expansion of British trade with China, they consistently refused to participate in attempts to put pressure on the government for intervention in the affairs of China or independent Burma. When an embassy from Burma visited England in 1872, the Liverpool Chamber of Commerce expressed its desire for an increase in Anglo-Burmese trade and urged the Burmese to cooperate with Britain in the opening of communications between British Burma and western China.[16] The Manchester Chamber of Commerce voiced a similar wish. The Manchester merchants also expressed their satisfaction over the government's decision to resume the survey of a route to western China in 1874.[17] But all this was a long way from pressing the British Government to interfere actively in the internal affairs of Upper Burma or China. This was made even clearer in 1872 when R. B. Shaw, British Trade Commissioner at Ladak, attempted to interest Liverpool and Manchester in western China, and again in 1873 when T. T. Cooper, a well-known explorer of Asia, pointed out the potentialities of northern Burma as a market for British goods. Lancashire businessmen were mildly interested in the possibilities. However, when they discovered that firm diplomatic action was required to secure the opening of ports and to prevent the exactions of local officials, they were remarkably reluctant to urge the government to undertake such free trade imperialism.[18]

If British merchants were generally indifferent to the Far East, they were even more apathetic towards the economic attractions of the 'Dark Continent' in the early 1870s. Where businessmen in the metropolis were concerned with African affairs in these years, it was usually in opposition to rather than in support of British interference in the internal affairs of independent African states and tribal polities. West Africa was the only part of the continent which attracted any significant attention in metropolitan commercial circles. Merchants in the West African trade sought the backing of commercial opinion in Britain in an attempt to press the British Government into intervening in the West African interior in the region of Lagos in the early 1870s. But even that area seemed to offer few economic opportunities, despite vigorous efforts by the West African merchants to stir up interest in metropolitan business circles.

Britain's administration of the Colony of Lagos in the years from 1865 to 1872 was an almost classic case of the colonial official working at cross purposes with the home authorities. John Glover, an energetic but sometimes impetuous young administrator with a military background, envisaged the Colony of Lagos essentially as a base from which British power could be extended over Yorubaland, the vast territory on whose coastline the small Colony was somewhat precariously situated. Neither the Foreign Office nor the Colonial Office were prepared to refrain from all interference in Yorubaland, despite the recommendations of a Select Committee of the House of Commons which, in 1865, came close to suggesting such a course. But Glover went too fast for the home authorities and his removal from office in 1872 brought the issue of intervention or restraint in West Africa to a head within the Colonial Office.[19]

British merchants in Lagos were by no means united in support of Glover's attempt to open new trading routes to the interior by a blockade of the mainland in 1872. Where merchants relied on African middlemen to bring produce to them, they opposed Glover's policy, which threatened their trading connections. Those merchants who hoped to benefit from the opening of alternate trade routes to the chief palm oil districts in the interior supported

Glover. Although the interventionists made a vigorous attempt to win the support of commercial opinion in Lancashire in the spring of 1877, their efforts were without success. Businessmen in Liverpool and Manchester were prepared to assist West African merchants to obtain increased representation in the legislative councils and greater efficiency in the administrations of the West African settlements but they adamantly refused to support proposals that seemed likely to involve the interference of the British Government with independent African states or tribal polities. Still less were they prepared to advocate the spending of imperial funds on the West African settlements.[20]

However, reluctance to encourage proposals which might increase Britain's responsibilities in West Africa did not mean that businessmen would have hastened to support the alienation of any of the existing settlements. When it became known in 1870 that the British Government was negotiating with France for the cession of the small riverain Colony of the Gambia in exchange for the consolidation of British interests on another part of the coast, there was a strong flurry of protest from British business circles. Merchants in Manchester and London opposed the transfer chiefly on the grounds that it was against the interests of both British and French merchants in the Colony as well as being disliked by the Africans, and that the change from English to French law would disrupt commerce. As it turned out, nothing came of the Gambia exchange negotiations in 1870, for the opposition which the Gambia merchants succeeded in arousing in the House of Commons persuaded the government not to proceed with the transfer without the consent of Parliament. With the coming of the Franco-Prussian war and the accession of Lord Kimberley to the Colonial Office, the negotiations with France were dropped, at least for the time being.[21]

Events in the rest of the African continent were virtually ignored by British commercial opinion in the early 1870s. In November 1870, for example, the Board of Trade sent the directors of the Manchester Chamber of Commerce a report by Consul Pakenham to the effect that there was a serious danger of British exports to Madagascar being displaced by American goods. But the Manchester merchants were not particularly alarmed by this prospect.[22] East Africa was not regarded as a sufficiently important market for Manchester to concern itself unduly with foreign competition there. With economic prospects in Europe and the other traditonal British markets so bright, remote and inaccessible regions like East Africa could offer few attractions to British businessmen.

Notes

[1] Percentages are calculated from the figures given by C. H. Feinstein, *National Income, Expenditure and Output of the United Kingdom 1855–1965*, Cambridge, 1972, Table 3, col. 2 and Table 4, col. 5.

[2] See, for examples, *Minutes of the Council of the Birmingham Chamber of Commerce* (hereafter *MBCC*), 27 July 1871; 2 Feb. 1872; 1 Aug. 1872. *Manchester Guardian* (hereafter *MG*), 31 Jan. 1871. *Liverpool Daily Courier* (hereafter *LDC*), 25 Jan. 1872.

[3] W. Schlote, *British Overseas Trade*, Oxford, 1952, p. 159.

[4] See, for example, *MG*, 24 Oct. 1871. *MBCC*, 2 Feb. 1872. *Report of the Association of Chambers of Commerce of the U.K.* (hereafter *RAAC*), 1871.

[5] P. Ashley, *Modern Tariff History*, London, 1920, pp. 307–11.

[6] Arthur Girault, *The Colonial Tariff Policy of France*, London, 1916, pp. 76–7.

[7] *MBCC*, 23 Aug. 1871; 18 Oct. 1871.

[8] *RACC*, Nov. 1869.

[9] Arthur Redford, *Manchester Merchants and Foreign Trade*, II, *1850–1939*, New York, 1967, p. 201.

[10] *LDC*, 20 May 1872.

[11] *Ibid.*

[12] *MG*, 12 March 1872; 26 June 1872.

[13] See Nathan A. Pelcovits, *Old China Hands and the Foreign Office*, New York, 1948, pp. 11–31, 20–65.

[14] See Mary C. Wright, *The Last Stand of Chinese Conservatism. The T'ung Chih Restoration, 1862 to 1874*, Stanford, California, 1957, pp. 279–90. Pelcovits, *Old China Hands*, pp. 71–4.

[15] A. R. Colquhoun and H. Hallett, *Report on the Railway Connection of Burma and China*, London, 1888.

[16] Dorothy Woodman, *The Making of Burma*, London, 1962, p. 192. *LDC*, 24 Aug. 1872.

[17] *MG*, 31 Oct. 1872; 1 Oct. 1874.

[18] *Proceedings of the Manchester Chamber of Commerce* (hereafter *PMCC*), 19 Nov. 1872. *MG*, 19 Dec. 1872; 22 April 1872. *Report of the Liverpool Chamber of Commerce* (hereafter *RLCC*), 1872.

[19] W. D. McIntyre, 'Commander Glover and the Colony of Lagos, 1861–1873', *Journal of African History* (hereafter *JAH*), iv, 1963, pp. 57–79. See also J. D. Hargreaves, *Prelude to the Partition of West Africa*, London, 1963, pp. 64–90.

[20] *PMCC*, 20 Nov. 1872; 13 Dec. 1872; 26 March 1872; 28 April 1873; 30 April 1873; 28 May 1873. *MG*, 1 Feb. 1873; 12 April 1873; 15 April 1873; 29 April 1873; 3 May 1873. *Liverpool Journal of Commerce* (hereafter *LJC*), 2 Aug. 1873. *LDC*, 25 Sept. 1873. *RLCC*, 1874.

[21] See Hargreaves, *Prelude* . . ., pp. 151–65.

[22] *PMCC*, 28 Dec. 1870.

Three

Economic recession and the first signs of a new commercial imperialism

From about 1873 to 1879 the British economy passed through a period of recession. Although the effects of the slump varied considerably among different trades and sometimes among different branches of the same trade, most sections of the economy suffered to some extent from the downswing. Recession began in 1873, when a series of economic crises in Europe and the United States led to a sharp decline in European and American demand for British goods. The immediate repercussions of these cutbacks for Britain's export trades depended largely on the extent to which they relied on European and American markets. The wool industry, for example, faced a severe demand shortage because of its heavy dependence on exports to Europe and the United States. For the same reason the iron and steel trades also suffered severely in the late seventies. On the other hand, the cotton industry escaped the initial impact of the slump because it exported such a large proportion of its output to Empire countries, particularly India, where a large expansion in demand in the late seventies tended to offset decreases elsewhere. But no industry was able totally to escape the consequences of the general decline in economic activity. Although the recession in the cotton trade was delayed until almost the end of the 1870s, cotton was in some respects hit hardest of all by the slump and many cotton merchants and manufacturers found themselves in a severe profit squeeze by 1878–9.

Between 1873 and 1879 gross domestic product fell by 10 per cent and total industrial production actually declined by 4 per cent from 1876 to 1879. Export values fell even more sharply, shrinking by 18 per cent between 1872 and 1879.[1] But figures alone do not convey the sense of frustration and alarm of businessmen in some of the depressed trades during these years. Many, if not most, merchants and manufacturers were unaware of the process of the trade cycle and they feared that the downswing in business activity might signal a permanent decline. Different remedies were put forward in business circles. Some businessmen hoped that a return of prosperity might be brought about by more energetic individual effort on the part of both employers and workers. Others urged the immediate reduction of wages. Still others saw the answer in the opening of new markets or even a return to protection.

The period 1876–86 marked a watershed in the development of the metallurgical trades of Birmingham. Before 1876 Britain's metallurgical industries enjoyed an almost unchallenged predominance in most of the world's markets; after 1886 British producers had to face increasingly severe foreign competition in overseas markets and in the home trade itself. Not all Birmingham trades were affected alike by the series of recessions which hit the country after 1875. Those industries which had developed most rapidly in the years from 1860 to 1875 weathered the difficult periods fairly well, either increasing their output or at least maintaining it during the period 1876–86. On the other hand, those trades which had barely been able to maintain themselves in the earlier years received an almost fatal blow with the onset of recession. Of the four great staples of Birmingham, the jewellery and brass trades fared best, showing a considerable independence of the cyclical fluctuations of trade. The small arms trade, however, which had been in difficulties before 1876, suffered severely during the recession. The button trade similarly went through a period of steady decline. The largest of the minor industries of Birmingham, the saddlery and harness trade, was able to maintain its output after 1876 largely because of the strength of export demand from the colonies. Likewise the manufacturers of edge tools enjoyed continued prosperity, at least up to 1885, because of a buoyant colonial market.[2]

As early as July 1874 the Council of the Birmingham Chamber of Commerce complained of falling prices, despite the large volume of trade in that year. By the end of 1876 the council was sufficiently alarmed over the fall in exports to summon a special general meeting of the Chamber to discuss the 'depressed state of trade'. The Birmingham merchants blamed the 'great and almost universal

23

depression' in business on the slump in Europe following the Franco-Prussian war, bad harvests, famines in India and China and a diminution in the American trade. They did not show any interest in the possibility of opening new markets in Africa as a remedy for the slump. When, in June 1877, the Royal Geographical Society requested the co-operation of the Birmingham Chamber of Commerce in the raising of an African Exploration Fund, the Chamber replied that the depression in the district's trade left little hope for the collection of money for such a purpose.[3]

Not all large commercial and industrial centres suffered as much as Birmingham. Since the ocean shipping trades enjoyed more or less continuous prosperity during the whole of the 1870s, Liverpool managed to escape most of the effects of the slump. The average level of earnings of Liverpool shipping lines after 1870 was generally maintained during years of recession and substantially increased in good years. If the tonnages handled by the port in the late seventies showed no great increase over the earlier half of the decade, they were at least maintained.[4] Although there were exceptions as some individual lines were forced to cut the number of their sailings and others reported considerable losses, the general feeling among businessmen in Liverpool was that complaints of depression in the shipping trades were much exaggerated. According to the President of the Liverpool Chamber of Commerce, the port passed 'very well through the depression', which he described as more a loss of profit than a loss of trade.[5]

Of the major commercial and industrial centres Manchester suffered most during the slump of the late seventies. The recession did not affect all branches of the cotton industry to the same extent, nor did its onset in the cotton trade coincide with conditions of slump in other industries. The coarse plain piece goods branch of the cotton industry was not severely affected because of the relative insignificance of American demand for this type of cloth. For plain goods India was the best market and a large increase in Indian consumption between 1874 and 1878 offset decreases in other markets. The printed and fancy goods section of the trade did not escape so lightly. Its chief market was in Central and South America, with the Empire and Europe coming together in second place; despite a rise in exports to the Empire, total exports of this type of cloth declined slightly.[6] The recession in the cotton trade was further complicated by the fact that the country as a whole began to recover from the slump before its sharpest impact was felt in the cotton industry.

The value of total exports of cotton goods fell from £80.2 million in 1872 to £64 million in 1879. This forced manufacturers to cut back sharply in production. Between 1874 and 1879 output of cotton yarn and cotton goods fell by 10 per cent and 13 per cent respectively.[7] More serious from the point of view of those engaged in the trade was the decline in the profitability of business in these years. The margin on 30's twist yarn, for example, fell from $5\frac{5}{8}d$. per pound to $2\frac{3}{8}d$. between October 1875 and July 1879.[8]

Although there were complaints of depressed trade from some cotton merchants and manufacturers in 1874, it was not until 1875–6 that the cotton manufacturing districts began to suffer seriously from the slump. In the north and north-east districts of Lancashire complaints of 'over-production' were heard frequently during 1876. As foreign demand slackened, the cotton spinners of Bolton, Preston, Burnley and Oldham resorted to wage cuts and short time in order to curtail production. On the whole, however, the outlook for the cotton industry was not particularly discouraging in 1876. Though many manufacturers complained of falling profits, it was generally hoped that the conclusion of free trade agreements with the major European industrial countries and a reduction of the Indian import duties would bring about an increase in the volume of business. But exports continued to shrink and towards the end of 1877 there was considerable industrial unrest when employers in north and north-east Lancashire proposed wage reductions, which the operatives were determined to resist unless the wage cuts were accompanied by a curtailment of production until trade revived. Strikes occurred throughout Lancashire in 1878 when employers demanded further wage reductions.[9]

It was in 1879 that the recession took its heaviest toll in the cotton manufacturing districts. In Preston alone in January it was estimated that about one thousand men were out of work. In Manchester, Salford, Preston and Bolton, applications for relief reached unprecedented numbers. Wage reductions and stoppages of production took place in all the cotton manufacturing centres, particularly in the Rossendale, Blackburn, Burnley, Preston, Oldham and Glossop districts. The slump was especially severe in Preston, where the Executive of the Weavers' Association of that town advised the operatives that the best thing they could do to alleviate the distress would be to emigrate in order to lessen the supply of labour. The universal complaint in the cotton manufacturing districts was 'over-production'.[10] Almost all the solutions which Manchester businessmen put forward for the relief of the economic distress had this much in common, that they were all designed to overcome an excess supply of manufactured goods.

Despite recession, most businessmen remained determined free-traders. Many hoped for a more liberal French tariff when the Cobden Treaty, renewed in 1873, came up for revision in 1877. Although there was great disappointment in business circles over the breakdown of the Anglo-French commercial treaty negotiations at the end of that year, few suggested retaliation as a means of forcing the French to liberalise their duties on British manufactures. At the end of 1878 the French Government formally denounced the Cobden Treaty and began to draw up a new general tariff. Since this took time to prepare, the treaty continued in effect for the time being. In the meantime, Spain introduced a new tariff containing higher duties on many British goods and tariff changes appeared to be imminent in Italy, Austria and Hungary. By 1879 British businessmen began to fear a general movement towards higher tariffs by many of Britain's traditional trading partners. However, the situation was still uncertain, for the issue of free trade versus protection appeared to be in the balance in France and its outcome in that country was regarded as crucial for the other continental nations.[11]

These free-trade issues of the late 1870s had important implications for British commerce outside the traditional European and American markets. In July 1877 the directors of the Manchester Chamber of Commerce learned that the Governor of the French African Colony of Senegal proposed to impose differential duties in favour of French manufactures. The directors immediately requested the Foreign Office to protest to the French Government.[12] They hoped that French colonial duties would be included in the negotiations with France for a new commercial treaty. With these suspended in 1877 and with the Senegal duties freshly before them, the directors had good reason to be pessimistic about the immediate future of free trade in France. The general trend towards protectionism in Europe was a potent argument for opening new markets in parts of the world where there were no hostile tariffs. Moreover, the French tariff in Senegal suggested that French colonial activities in Africa and Asia could threaten British trade in regions where new markets might be found. Although it was not until the 1880s that such arguments gained wide currency in British commercial circles,[13] they began to be heard during the late 1870s and above all in Manchester, where the severity of the recession gave them increased urgency.

Few businessmen looked towards the colonies of settlement for relief from the economic slump. Indeed, now that the country was suffering from recession, the settlement colonies were more unpopular than ever in British commercial circles. With her protectionist tariff policy Canada gave the greatest offence during these years and to many British businessmen she showed colonial ingratitude at its worst. While merchants in Birmingham, Glasgow, Liverpool, London and Manchester all complained of colonial tariffs, they had by the late seventies reluctantly come to accept the fact that the British Government could do little beyond persuasion to make the errant colonies mend their ways.[14] The new Canadian tariff of 1879 resulted in even higher duties on many British exports and led to bitter complaints from metropolitan merchants that the Canadian tariff was more unfavourable to the mother country than the tariffs of France and Germany.[15]

India offered a far more promising field for British businessmen in the second half of the 1870s. India remained the largest single consumer of British cotton textiles throughout the whole period from 1870 to 1895. Yet even here there were dark clouds on the horizon. By the late 1870s Lancashire was beginning to fear a growing divergence between the economic interests of Britain and her Far Eastern dependency. The Indian cotton manufacturing industry had made considerable strides since the first cotton mill was built at Bombay in 1853. The construction of railways after 1857 and the opening of the Suez Canal in 1869 made bulk transport feasible for the first time. If this intensified competition for Indian manufactures, it also greatly lowered the import costs of capital goods. The products of Indian mills began to compete with Manchester goods before the 1870s but it was only after about 1874 that this was regarded with serious concern by Lancashire merchants and manufacturers. This concern resulted in a commercial campaign for the abolition of the Indian duties on imported cotton goods and yarns. These duties had been imposed for revenue purposes in the 1860s but falling prices had greatly increased their incidence on Lancashire goods by the early 1870s and British cotton interests began to complain that they acted as a protective tariff for the Indian cotton industry. Led by Manchester, businessmen mounted a campaign to force the British Government to abolish the duties.[16]

The timing of the 1875 to 1879 anti-duties campaign has a broader significance for, as we shall see, Manchester's reaction to Indian industrialisation had an important effect on its attitude towards market opportunities in Africa. In response to commercial pressure in 1874–5 the British Government instructed the Government of India to fix a date for the abolition of the duties. The Indian Government was highly reluctant to lose the revenues from the duties, although these amounted to only a small proportion of its total income, and high Indian government officials procrastinated over their abolition. The partial exemptions granted by the Government of India in 1878 served only to stimulate Manchester to press harder for total abolition. Finally, in March 1879, after tremendous pressure was put on the British Government by the cotton interests, the Government of India was obliged to abolish the duties on all goods made of yarns coarser than 30's count. Since Indian production was largely restricted to this class of goods, the government hoped that the exemptions would remove the protective character of the duties. Although Manchester was not completely satisfied with the situation in 1879, the exemptions did for a time silence complaints about 'unfair' Indian competition in the cotton industry.

The recession of the late 1870s did not produce any strong mercantile pressure for the opening of new markets in the Far East. Despite vigorous efforts by the China merchants to stir up interest in commercial circles, British businessmen remained generally apathetic towards commercial prospects in China. A serious situation in Anglo-Chinese relations arose in January 1875 when a British consul was murdered in Chinese territory, an incident that could easily have led to a major Anglo-Chinese confrontation. This of course was exactly what the China merchants were hoping for and they made the most of the opportunity to press for direct British intervention in China. The merchants claimed that the Chinese Government's delay in apprehending those responsible for the consul's death was damning proof of the corruption and inefficiency of the Peking regime. They demanded that the British

Government use the occasion to force major reforms upon the Chinese, including the opening of much more of the interior to foreign trade.[17]

The British Government's investigation into the incident culminated in the conclusion of the Chefoo Convention in September 1876. The new agreement sought not only to settle the 1875 murder but also to regulate political and commercial intercourse between the Chinese and foreigners. For the China merchants, however, it was another 'betrayal' by the British Government. The merchants hoped at least for a more aggressive British policy and a new treaty which would provide for significant fiscal and administrative changes in the Chinese provinces. Arguing that China was a valuable market whose development was being held up by 'corrupt' mandarins, they sought to gain the support of commercial opinion in Britain for a policy of direct pressure on the Chinese provincial authorities. But once again they were unsuccessful. While most British businessmen would have welcomed the creation of a new market in the Far East, it was not to that part of the world that they naturally looked for the extension of overseas trade. And they remained adamantly opposed to government intervention in places like China.[18]

Africa was regarded in much the same light. Increased trade with that continent would be desirable but Africa held a very low priority in British business circles. There was little interest in the commercial possibilities of tropical Africa and no mercantile pressure on the government for interference in the 'confusing' world of African politics. However, although businessmen in the leading commercial and industrial centres were generally indifferent to the economic attractions of Africa, the recession of the late 1870s marked the beginnings of an important change in mercantile attitudes towards the 'Dark Continent'. For the first time since the Industrial Revolution, significant metropolitan business interests gave serious attention to the market possibilities of tropical Africa. Commercial interest in Africa in 1879 emanated from the industry that was most severely affected by recession, the cotton trade. Moreover within the cotton trade it was from those manufacturing districts which suffered most in 1878–9 that African schemes originated.

It was in Preston, of all Lancashire towns one of those most severely affected by the slump, that James Bradshaw[19] put forward

his plan for the alleviation of the distress in the cotton manufacturing districts by the creation of a new market in Central
Africa. Bradshaw had attempted to arouse Manchester's interest in
Africa in 1876 but although he attracted some attention, his efforts
met with little success at the time. In 1879, however, conditions
were more favourable for the reception of his scheme—outlined at
a crowded meeting of employers and operatives in Preston in
December 1878—for the opening of Central Africa by a railway
from Zanzibar. Bradshaw had no detailed plan in mind at the time,
his purpose being to bring the general idea before the commercial
public before working out the details. The commercial penetration
of Central Africa would be undertaken as a national enterprise and
all classes were invited to participate; working people could become
involved through the creation of £1 shares. Though it was to be a
national effort, it would be strictly an affair of private enterprise:
'They did not want it to become a Government affair, because that
might create jealousy on the part of other nations . . .'[20] Benefits
would not be restricted to the cotton trade: 'The opening out of
Africa would not only benefit Lancashire, but the hardware trades
of Sheffield and Birmingham'.[21] The 'scheme' was really a kind of
spontaneous response to acute economic distress, as is clear from
the almost chimerical nature of some of its objects:

> If their object [i.e. the opening up of Central Africa] could be
> carried out by some means, it would not only be a benefit to
> Lancashire in her cotton trade, but to all trades that were
> directly or indirectly connected with it, and they would
> experience great prosperity for many years to come.[22]

Bradshaw pointed out the particular advantages of a market in
Africa:

> Because our Indian market had only probably been acquired
> by reason of the fact that we were able to produce cotton
> cheaper than the natives of India themselves, who had a
> physical capacity for the work, and had been spinners for ages.
> This might not always be the case, and hence the advantage of
> opening a trade in Africa, where there were millions of people
> who had no capacity for skilled labour.[23]

An organising committee of employers and operatives was
appointed to publicise the aims of the promoters.

During the early months of 1879 Bradshaw was instrumental in organising public meetings in a number of the depressed districts of Lancashire. The same kind of spontaneous reaction to economic adversity was evident at a crowded meeting in the town hall of Blackburn in March. The Mayor to the town presided and a resolution was enthusiastically adopted,

> that the meeting was of opinion that the continent of Africa presented a favourable field for the development and extension of British commerce, and especially of the cotton trade, and it invited the support of capitalists in opening up the country and pledged itself to do all in its power to promote the realization of the scheme.[24]

Bradshaw also brought his plan before the Society of Arts in London and, later in the year, attempted to interest the Trades Union Congress in Edinburgh. He sent circulars to bank managers, leading members of chambers of commerce and some forty or fifty prominent Manchester businessmen to advertise his ideas.[25] The greatest response to his efforts came from the depressed districts of Lancashire.

By the winter of 1878–9 the serious distress in the cotton manufacturing districts, increasing fear of Indian competition and great uncertainty over the future of British trade in traditional European markets turned the attention of many Manchester businessmen towards the idea of opening new overseas markets as the remedy for their economic problems. The Manchester Chamber of Commerce became indirectly involved in African schemes in January 1879 when F. W. Grafton, a calico printer of Manchester and a prominent member of the Chamber, presided at a public meeting organised by Bradshaw in Manchester. Although Grafton said that he would not go to the extent of describing Africa as our 'second India' as Bradshaw had called it, he agreed with those who urged its opening to commerce because of the imperative need to create new markets. The first thing, however, Grafton stressed, would be to collect and disseminate information on the whole subject so that the public could be educated on Africa.[26]

The importance of opening new markets was also pointed out by the President of the Manchester Chamber of Commerce at the Chamber's annual meeting a few days later:

> In view . . . of the retrograde movement on the part of the

various countries of Europe and the United States, whereby markets were becoming closed to us, was it not our duty to take part in and stimulate any well-matured enterprise for the purpose of opening new markets and establishing commercial alliances with the peoples of less civilized countries, which had yet been but partially explored.[27]

Referring to the opening of Central Africa, he reiterated Grafton's caution: 'Proper means of communications must be made, competent persons must go out to survey and open routes, and to construct roads or even railways'.[28] Despite their initial reserve, the Manchester directors were sufficiently interested to convene a special meeting of the Manchester Chamber of Commerce on 21 February 1879 to consider the problems of opening Africa to British commerce. Most of the directors attended, as did the Bishop of Salford and a number of merchants trading to West Africa, including James F. Hutton, a prominent Manchester West Africa merchant. It was almost certainly through Hutton's initiative that several persons considered to be impartial 'experts' on Africa were invited to the meeting. These were F. Holmwood, Her Majesty's Assistant Political Agent at Zanzibar, Captain Foot, R.N., and Mr E. Jenkins, M.P. With their practical knowledge of conditions in Africa, Holmwood and Foot could be expected to help shape a more definite plan to open up the country along the lines suggested by Bradshaw.

Jenkins outlined a plan to the Manchester merchants for obtaining a concession from the Government of Zanzibar for the construction of a railway through the Sultan's mainland possessions from Dar es Salaam. The Sultan, he said, was willing to grant a railway concession in return for the payment of a certain sum towards the revenues of Zanzibar. The railway could be easily and cheaply constructed and would carry Manchester goods into the interior and bring back native produce. Both Holmwood and Foot made a special point of emphasising that their plans would involve no fighting and no annexations. The directors set up a committee to confer with the promoters on the implementation of these plans.[29]

In reality the proposals outlined by Jenkins were as chimerical as those of Bradshaw. Although the promoters reported that the Sultan's authority on the mainland extended from 30 to 100 miles from the coastline, they proposed to construct a railway to an unstated destination 250 miles inland. There were no grounds for believing that the Sultan would have been prepared to grant a concession at that time and the promoters had only the haziest notions of the kinds of commodities they might obtain in exchange for manufactured goods.[30] Moreover, some of the directors of the Manchester Chamber of Commerce were highly sceptical about the whole idea of finding new markets in tropical Africa. John Slagg, an influential Manchester cloth merchant and Liberal politician, pointed out to the Chamber's Board of Directors that there might be new markets much more accessible than East Africa. He was very doubtful about the ability of Europeans to survive the African climate and he particularly deprecated any notion of annexations.

The Manchester directors were first and foremost practical businessmen. They would not turn their backs on any possibility of opening new markets, especially during a time of severe recession in the cotton trade. On the other hand, they would not risk their reputations, let alone their capital, by giving unqualified support to large enterprises where the likelihood of success was highly problematical. They did not go to the government for assistance; in fact they specifically ruled out the idea of state intervention in African ventures. Instead, they adopted a typically mid-Victorian solution, suggested by the Bishop of Salford at the directors' meeting with Holmwood in February: they decided to found a Society for the Study of Commercial Geography! Its main purpose, according to the Mayor of Manchester who presided at the founding meeting in March 1879, was

> to inaugurate a movement in the face of our declining commerce, to see whether some other large sectors of the human race could not be brought into commercial intercourse with this manufacturing country. The present condition of trade certainly required all who occupied public positions, and those who had capital invested in manufacturing concerns, to consider whether anything could be done to promote the revival of trade which they all hoped for, but of which at present there were very few signs. The idea in the minds of those who had moved in the matter was that there should be a new society formed whose operations should be somewhat beyond the ordinary operations of Chambers of Commerce and that scientific and geographical researches should be made in

different parts of the globe with the view of discovering fresh fields for the commerce of this country.[31]

However, interest in the commercial development of Central Africa was already waning in Manchester. The Geographical Society at first received the support of the Manchester merchants in its appeal for funds but it met with little success after the first half of 1879 and was shortly afterwards wound up. Its successor, the Manchester Geographical Society, did not hold its inaugural meeting until January 1885. In Manchester commercial circles little more was heard of Central Africa after about the middle of 1879. There were several reasons for this. First, in March 1879 the Manchester merchants were informed by the India Office that the Government of India had agreed to remit the import duties on many Manchester goods which competed with the productions of the Indian mills. The Manchester Chamber of Commerce had demanded this exemption in March of the preceding year; in the autumn of 1878 and during the first two months of 1879, in conjunction with organisations of working men and employers throughout Lancashire, the Manchester Chamber had participated in a massive campaign for the abolition of the Indian cotton duties. Although they continued to demand the total repeal of the Indian duties, the Manchester merchants admitted that the concessions of March gave them considerable satisfaction. They confidently looked forward to substantial increases in cotton exports to India. Secondly, and more important, a revival of trade definitely set in during the last half of 1879, first in chemicals, then in steel, cotton and other industries. Already in May 1879, when signs of improvement appeared, the Manchester merchants began to consider whether it might not be impractical to look for new markets in regions as distant and inaccessible as East Africa. As President Ashworth told the Manchester Chamber, 'we were trying to open up a market amongst a lot of barbarians in Africa, while in Spain [because of the Spanish tariff] there were millions of civilized subjects to whom our goods were practically prohibited from being sent'.[32] He suggested that instead of vague African schemes Britain should attempt to extend her markets in Europe. A good place to start, he thought, would be to work for a new Anglo-Spanish trade agreement which would remove the then-existing difficulties in the way of increased trade between Britain and Spain.

From the end of 1879 to about 1883 the British economy passed through an expansionary phase. Export values increased by 23 per cent in these years, while gross domestic product rose 14 per cent between 1879 and 1882.[33] As the revival of late 1879 continued into the following year, the general climate of business opinion passed from pessimism to mild optimism. Businessmen hoped that the economy would now resume its upward course following the strange aberrations of the late seventies.

From about 1880 to the middle of 1882 the most important single subject of discussion in British commercial circles was the negotiations between Britain and France for a new commercial treaty. These negotiations, suspended in 1877 pending the preparation of a new French general tariff, were renewed in June 1880. British businessmen were highly optimistic that the renewal of tariff discussions would lead to the conclusion of a new Anglo-French commercial treaty which would not only bring about greatly increased trade between Britain and France but also set an example for the rest of Europe to follow. Despite signs of growing protectionist feeling in France, British commercial opinion tended to believe that the free-trade movement in that country was still in the ascendant. The Executive of the Association of U.K. Chambers of Commerce reported at the beginning of 1880 that 'it appears from evident hesitation in certain quarters on the continent [that] an indiscriminate increase of duties abroad is not so easy of accomplishment as once supposed'.[34]

These sanguine expectations were short-lived. The new French tariff of 1881 represented a general increase of about 24 per cent on the previous rates. The Anglo-French tariff negotiations were terminated in February 1882 when Britain and France reverted to a most-favoured-nation arrangement instead of a commercial treaty.[35] The new French tariff of the previous year, which came into effect in May 1882, contributed to a decline in France's share of Britain's exports in the 1880s, but this resulted less from the tariff itself than from the general stagnation of the French economy in that decade.[36] Although France did not revert to extreme protection until the early 1890s, the tariff of 1881 marked a turning point after which French officials and businessmen became increasingly protectionist. For commercial opinion in Britain the significance of the new French tariff and the failure to secure a free-trade treaty with France were profound. With the most liberal nation in Europe turning its back on free trade, there appeared to be little hope for that principle in other European countries. Together with a severe economic recession in the mid 1880s, the French protectionist revival was to contribute to a change in the bias and preference of British businessmen away from the traditional European markets and to create strong interest in opening new and hitherto neglected regions of the world to British trade. For the moment however this change was delayed by the upswing in economic activity in the early 1880s.

The economic difficulties of the late seventies had led to a rise of protectionist feeling in some manufacturing centres in Britain. Sheffield, Bradford, Bristol, Dewsbury, Huddersfield, Birmingham and Wolverhampton all produced protectionist movements, though in most cases these were of comparatively minor significance.[37] In its early stages the protectionist movement broadened into demands for some form of fiscal union between the mother country and the colonies. The initiative in this development came chiefly from the larger settlement colonies, particularly Canada, where influential commercial associations like the Dominion Board of Trade in Montreal began to advocate a commercial union of the colonies and Britain. But apart from Birmingham and a few other industrial centres where protectionist sentiments had gained a foothold, the idea of a commercial union of the Empire found few adherents in the British business world.[38]

With the abolition of a large part of the Indian cotton duties in the spring of 1879 and a general brightening of Britain's economic prospects in 1880, mercantile opinion was much less concerned with Indian affairs than in the late 1870s. However, Manchester continued to press for the total abolition of the Indian cotton duties. The Manchester Chamber of Commerce argued that the remaining duties, which were on the finer classes of goods, would stimulate the Indian mills to produce the finer products. Although Manchester had lost considerable ground in the sale of the coarser types of cotton goods in the Indian market, English cloth continued to enjoy a virtual monopoly of the market for higher quality cottons. Since the Manchester merchants believed that the protective nature of the Indian cotton duties had given rise to Indian production of the coarser cloth, they feared that Indian manufacturers would now shift their efforts to take advantage of the shelter afforded by the remaining duties and that Indian competition might develop in the market for the finer cottons. The final abolition of the duties in the spring of 1882 was greeted with great jubilation in commercial circles in Britain and led many businessmen to predict a speedy decline of cotton manufacturing in India. In this they were of course mistaken, though it took another four or five years before it became apparent that Indian competition was something Lancashire would have to learn to live with.

There were some signs of increased mercantile interest in the Far East and renewed agitation for the construction of a railway between British Burma and western China towards the end of 1882. But this, as we shall see, was directly associated with another recession which began to affect the British economy towards the end of that year.

Apart from the west coast of the African continent, there was little interest in Africa in the early 1880s. The West African trade was of particular value to Lancashire, since, as the President of the Manchester Chamber of Commerce said in November 1880, 'they would have no hostile tariffs to deal with as they had with many other countries more advanced in civilization'.[39] While the Manchester directors might press the Colonial Office for alterations in the commercial law in certain of the West African settlements, there was no thought of extending British influence in these regions: 'They did not want annexations or conquests in West Africa',[40] stressed the President of the Manchester Chamber of Commerce in 1880. The Liverpool merchants were no more eager for the extension of British influence in West Africa, as the Liverpool Chamber of Commerce made clear in 1880 when they rejected suggestions that Liverpool lend its support to proposals for the construction of light railways in the Gold Coast.[41] It was not until they were faced with a severe business slump and a great intensification of foreign competition in the mid 1880s that significant numbers of British businessmen began to turn their attention towards Africa.

Notes

[1] Calculated from C. H. Feinstein, *National Income, Expenditure and Output of the United Kingdom 1855–1965*, Table 3, col. 2; Table 4, col. 5; Table 51, col. 1.

² This paragraph is based largely on G. C. Allen, *The Industrial Development of Birmingham and the Black Country 1860–1927*, New York, 1966, p. 212.

³ *Report of the Council of the Birmingham Chamber of Commerce* (hereafter *RBCC*), 1874. *MBCC*, 18 Oct. 1876; 25 Feb. 1878; 28 Feb. 1879; 27 June 1877.

⁴ F. E. Hyde, *Liverpool and the Mersey*, Liverpool, 1971, pp. 100–3.

⁵ *LDC*, 12 April 1877; 7 Jan. 1878; 3 July 1877; 31 Oct. 1877; 3 Nov. 1877; 11 Feb. 1879.

⁶ S. B. Saul, *Studies in British Overseas Trade, 1870–1914*, Liverpool, 1960, pp. 100–2.

⁷ B. R. Mitchell and P. Deane, *Abstract of British Historical Statistics*, London, 1962, Table 8, p. 304. W. G. Hoffman, *British Industry, 1700–1950*, New York, 1965, Table 54, Part B, cols. 28, 29.

⁸ The margin in cotton spinning is the difference between the price of raw cotton and the price of yarn: in weaving it is the difference between the price of yarn and that of cloth. The margin includes all costs of production, wages and profits. See R. E. Tyson, 'The Cotton Industry', in D. H. Aldcroft (ed.), *The Development of British Industry and Foreign Competition 1875–1914*, London, 1968, p. 102.

⁹ *MG*, 3 June 1876; 1 Jan. 1877; 15 Jan. 1877; 12 Dec. 1877; 19 April 1878; 23 April 1878; 1 May 1878; 2 May 1878; 21 June 1878; 1 Jan. 1879. See also T. Ellison, *The Cotton Trade in Great Britain*, London, 1886, p. 107.

¹⁰ *MG*, 1 Jan. 1879; 6 Jan. 1879; 9 Jan. 1879; 1 April 1879; 14 Aug. 1879; 23 Aug. 1879; 11 Oct. 1879.

¹¹ S. B. Clough, *France. A History of National Economics 1789–1939*, New York, 1939, pp. 215–16. *LJC*, 5 Nov. 1877; 18 Jan. 1878. *LDC*, 6 Feb. 1877. *RBCC*, 1878. *RACC*, Feb. 1878; March 1879. *Minutes of the Board of Directors of the Glasgow Chamber of Commerce* (hereafter *MGCC*), 10 Feb. 1879. *PMCC*, 19 Feb. 1879. *MG*, 20 Feb. 1879.

¹² *PMCC*, 27 June 1877. See also C. W. Newbury, 'The Protectionist Revival in French Colonial Trade: The Case of Senegal', *Economic History Review* (hereafter *EcHR*), xxi, pp. 331–48.

¹³ See below.

¹⁴ See, for example, *MGCC*, 14 April 1879. *MBCC*, 18 June 1879; 4 June 1879; 15 Oct. 1879. *RACC*, Feb. 1876; Feb. 1878. *MG*, 2 Feb. 1877; 24 April 1878; 7 May 1878; 6 May 1879. *LDC*, 6 Feb. 1877.

[15] See Saul, *Studies in British Overseas Trade*, Ch. 6. Also *MBCC*, 18 June 1879; 4 June 1879. *MGCC*, 14 April 1879.

[16] See P. Harnetty, *Imperialism and Free Trade: Lancashire and India in the Mid-Nineteenth Century*, Vancouver, 1972, pp. 32–4; E. C. Moulton, *Lord Northbrook's Indian Administration 1872–76*, London, 1968, pp. 174–214; A. Redford, *Manchester Merchants and Foreign Trade*, II, *1850–1939*, New York, 1967, pp. 21–31.

[17] S. T. Wang, *The Margary Affair and the Chefoo Agreement*, Oxford, 1940, esp. pp. 45–53, 73, 111–15.

[18] Pelcovits, *Old China Hands and the Foreign Office*, pp. 122–4, 129–30.

[19] Bradshaw was a representative of the firm of Horrockses, Crewdson and Co. Ltd, cotton spinners and manufacturers at Preston and Bolton.

[20] *MG*, 2 Jan. 1879.

[21] *Ibid.*

[22] *Ibid.*

[23] *Ibid.*

[24] *MG*, 13 March 1879.

[25] *MG*, 20 March 1879; 16 June 1879.

[26] *MG*, 8 Jan. 1879.

[27] *MG*, 4 Feb. 1879.

[28] *Ibid.*

[29] *PMCC*, 21 Feb. 1879. *MG*, 24 Feb. 1879.

[30] See J. S. Galbraith, *Mackinnon and East Africa 1878–95. A Study in the New Imperialism*, Cambridge, 1972, esp. pp. 74–5.

[31] *MG*, 13 March 1879.

[32] 6 May 1879.

[33] Calculated from Feinstein, *National Income, Expenditure and Output*, Table 3, col. 2; Table 4, col. 5.

[34] *RACC*, Feb. 1880.

[35] Clough, *France. A History of National Economics*, p. 217.

[36] See W. L. Thorp, *Business Annals*, New York, 1926, pp. 191–2.

[37] B. H. Brown, *The Tariff Reform Movement in Great Britain 1881–95*, New York, 1943, pp. 9–28.

[38] See, for examples, *PMCC*, 9 Feb. 1881. *MGCC*, 22 Dec. 1880. *LJC*, 1 Feb. 1881. *LDC*, 22 Feb. 1881. *RACC*, Feb. 1880; Oct. 1881.

[39] *MG*, 23 Nov. 1880.

[40] *Ibid.*

[41] *RLCC*, 1880.

Four

The business slump of the mid 1880s: transition to the imperialism of free trade

One of the most severe slumps of the late nineteenth century hit the British economy between about 1883 and 1886. Despite great unevenness in its effects, the recession gave rise to the widespread belief that there existed a disproportion between the productive capacity of the industrialised countries of the world and effective world demand for manufactured goods. Although this notion was not restricted to businessmen, it was in commercial circles that it was most widely expressed. Different remedies were put forward to alleviate the recession, most of them working on the assumption that supply and demand would somehow have to be brought back into balance, either by curtailment of supply or enlargement of demand or both.

Many businessmen believed that the best remedy for the pre-vailing recession was the stimulation of demand by opening new export markets. For a time it was hoped that new outlets could be developed entirely under non-official auspices. Private enterprise would rise to the occasion and create new markets in areas of the world not then open to British trade. However, the deepening of the recession, the assistance given by foreign governments to their merchants and industrialists and the threatening prospect that protectionist European powers would carve out exclusive spheres of influence in Africa and Asia made it seem less likely that indivi-dual enterprise in Britain would receive its just reward without the help of government. British merchants began to call upon the government for greater aid to overseas trade. Their chief objective was still the extension of free-trade markets but from about the middle of the 1880s free trade seemed to require ever-increasing degrees of intervention abroad. There was a shift in mercantile attitudes towards then-unexploited regions in tropical Africa and Asia. The indifference of the 1870s was replaced in the mid 1880s by commercial demands for the promotion of free trade in tropical Africa and Asia by active political intervention.

In the spring of 1883 the Birmingham Chamber of Commerce complained of a general tendency for productive power to outrun demand and for competition to increase. There was consequently, the Chamber declared, 'great and increasing difficulty in finding remunerative markets and obtaining an adequate profit for the skill and capital employed'.[1] Of the staple trades of Birmingham, the small arms industry suffered most in the mid 1880s. With the Franco-Prussian war and the changeover from the large bore to the small bore rifle in the early 1870s, the industry underwent a great expansion in productive capacity. After the early 1870s, a period of peace and stability of design led to a sharp decline in demand. Competition became increasingly severe, for by the late 1870s the leading European powers set up their own factories for military arms and the Enfield Company's production was sufficient to meet the peace-time requirements of the British armed forces. Moreover, the gunsmiths of Belgium were able to produce sporting guns and African muskets more cheaply than Birmingham makers. In 1871 the trade had employed 8,200 persons in Staffordshire and Warwickshire, a number that in 1881 had fallen by over 3,000.[2]

Throughout the mid 1880s the Birmingham merchants pressed the British Government to seek reductions in foreign tariffs, which they believed were one of the main causes of the slump. However, there was little that British Governments could do to persuade European countries to forego their duties on imports of manufactured goods. This led some Birmingham businessmen to look towards neutral or hitherto unexploited regions of the world. Africa was regarded as a potentially valuable market where protective tariffs were largely non-existent. The small arms manufacturers of Birmingham in particular looked to Africa as a much-needed outlet for muskets and cheap sporting guns.[3]

Although 1885 brought a burst of prosperity to the Birmingham small arms manufacturers, largely as a result of the threatened hostilities between Russia and England in that year, for the Birmingham area as a whole the slump bottomed out in 1885. The Birmingham Chamber of Commerce continued to advocate the opening of new markets as a remedy for recession but there was no unanimity among Birmingham businessmen on ways of restoring prosperity to the district's trade. After 1885 protectionism steadily gained ground in Birmingham when it became linked with plans for imperial federation, which the Birmingham Chamber hoped would bring a solution for the twin problems of overproduction and foreign competition.

In Glasgow the slump of the mid eighties affected all sections of trade and industry with the single exception of shipbuilding. Complaints during these years were not so much over the depressed volume of trade as the smallness of profits and in some cases of the unprofitability of business. Like the Birmingham merchants, the directors of the Glasgow Chamber of Commerce attributed the trouble largely to an 'excess of production at home and abroad'.

Despite the slump, advocates of retaliation and reciprocity got little sympathy in Glasgow business circles. The protective duties of foreign countries were admittedly a burden for British producers and merchants in many ways but there was also a positive side to the picture. It was argued by some Glasgow businessmen that universal free trade would not in fact be in Britain's true interest at all. The high cost of the exports of the protectionist countries prevented them from effectively competing with British goods in the neutral markets of the world. As the President of the Glasgow Chamber of Commerce pointed out in 1882, universal free trade would be 'certain to bring competition into foreign markets where at present it is not known'.[4] The neutral markets of the world were the chief hope for a free-trading Britain and it was to these that the Glasgow Chamber of Commerce turned increasingly for the further extension of British trade after about the middle of the 1880s. If the preservation of free trade abroad appeared to demand an interventionist foreign policy, the Glasgow merchants were not slow to bring pressure upon the government. As we shall see below, they began to demand British interference in both Africa and the Far East.

Liverpool escaped the worst effects of the slump of the mid 1880s. The steady increase in the figures of net registered tonnage using the port throughout this period would suggest that there was not much correlation between the volume of Liverpool shipping and cyclical fluctuations in British production and trade. But there was an additional factor that led Liverpool businessmen to favour intervention in 'undeveloped' areas abroad, particularly in West Africa, from about the middle of the 1880s.

The 1880s saw a steady increase in the numbers and influence of African merchants in Liverpool. Most of these merchants were engaged in the West African trade, purchasing palm oil and supplying manufactured goods, chiefly cottons, liquor and firearms. Many of the smaller firms were fighting for a share of the trade in a highly competitive market and they resented attempts by the older established houses to restrict trading to the coastal regions. Some of the more enterprising larger firms, like that of John Holt of Liverpool,[5] also had their eyes on the interior. Then there were the growing number of Liverpool commission houses, which bought and sold goods for merchants along the whole of the African coast. The commission houses could expect to profit from an enlargement of the market by the opening of the interior. Similarly the African steamship companies, prominent in the Liverpool Chamber of Commerce, could count on increased business by a widening of the market.[6] In general all the British West African merchants were highly fearful of attempts by their European competitors to obtain exclusive trading privileges. Despite competition among themselves, British West African merchants frequently co-operated with one another on matters affecting the trade as a whole. Their chief lobby, the West African Section of the Liverpool Chamber of Commerce, founded in 1884, became one of the most powerful commercial associations in Liverpool by the end of the decade.

The recession was a major preoccupation of merchants in London in the mid 1880s. One of the chief concerns of the London Chamber of Commerce at its founding in 1882 was the problem of 'over-production'. As a remedy the London Chamber urged the opening of new markets in areas of the world 'hitherto neglected'. The Chamber's widely-read *Journal*, under the editorship of its Secretary, Kenric B. Murray, quickly developed into one of the most influential advocates of the creation of new overseas markets as the solution to economic recession:

> There are not buyers simultaneously for our extended production and of that which the rapid development of the industrial capacity of a majority of other nations has thrown on the world's markets. Everybody has been building mills and workshops, nobody has given his attention to training of tribes and nations to become new buyers, and so we have drifted rapidly into the present period of plethory.[7]

There appeared to be two possible solutions to recession, as the London Chamber's *Journal* pointed out in May 1884: 'The one would be a repetition in Central Africa of the action which founded our Indian Empire. The other, a movement of concentration and consolidation of our present possessions'.[8] Both solutions were canvassed by the London Chamber of Commerce in the 1880s, but the main emphasis was placed on the opening of new markets. The *Journal* called upon businessmen to 'prepare public opinion, and the Government of the country for a new colonial movement from which alone a revival of trade can be expected'.[9]

Manchester became the strongest advocate of new overseas markets in the 1880s. Recession hit the cotton industry in the middle of a minor boom. A huge American cotton crop in 1882 led to a sharp decline in raw cotton prices and caused heavy speculative buying in 1882–3. The output of cotton yarn and cotton goods, both of which had been steadily increasing since 1879, rose by almost 5 per cent for yarn and 3 per cent for goods between 1882 and 1883.[10] As 1883 advanced and previous contracts for deliveries of goods expired, spinners and manufacturers found that new orders could not be obtained except at unprofitable rates because of the low demand in most foreign markets. There were frequent complaints of over-production in the cotton manufacturing districts in the early months of 1883. As margins in both spinning and weaving declined, shut-downs occurred. By the end of 1883 it was estimated that some 50,000 to 60,000 looms were idle.[11]

Although the directors of the Manchester Chamber of Commerce were in general agreement that the main problem was an over-production of goods, there was at first no unanimity over a solution. Some believed the only remedy was a curtailment of production until demand revived. This was unpopular, however, for restricting production tended to drive up costs. Wage reductions were a favoured resort of employers in times of recession but wage cuts were usually accompanied by the distressing side-effect of labour unrest. Towards the end of 1883 the Employers' Association of North and North-East Lancashire reached agreement on a 5 per cent reduction in the wages of weavers. But the operatives struck against the proposed 'remedy' and demanded that the government set up a Royal Commission to inquire into the distress in the cotton industry.[12]

A widely-canvassed solution to depression was the development of new overseas markets to absorb the increased output of the cotton industry. This was stressed by John Slagg, a prominent member of the Manchester Chamber of Commerce, in May 1882. Slagg had earlier prepared a report for the Manchester merchants on the protectionist movement in France and like many British merchants he was far from sanguine over the future of free trade in Europe. Without much hope for relief from that quarter, Slagg was 'always impressed, when discussing the ups and downs of trade, with the vast importance of the development of additional markets'. The cotton industry, he feared, had overstocked its markets, 'the result being loss to themselves and privation to their workpeople'.[13] A slump in the Indian trade in 1882–3 temporarily dampened hopes for relief from that direction and together with the stagnation in other overseas markets led the Manchester merchants seriously to consider the possibility of opening up a vast new market in China.

During the first half of 1884, cotton output was reduced by an extensive strike against wage reductions in the Blackburn, Darwen and Padiham districts. Despite the decreased output brought about by the strike, it was estimated that margins in the cotton industry during the years 1884–5 fell to the lowest levels that contemporaries could recall. The belief that 'over-production' was at the root of the trouble was very widespread. Even *The Economist* agreed in early 1885 that 'in all directions, especially in countries where protective tariffs have caused a hothouse growth in certain industries, productive capacity has outstripped the growth of population. In other words, supply has outrun demand'.[14]

For the cotton trade the slump bottomed out in 1885. Production cuts and strikes against proposed wage reductions made the outlook for cotton bleak indeed in 1884–5. For many businessmen the problem was clear:

> If any proof is required that the augmented rate of production had outrun any increase that might reasonably have been expected in the rate of consumption, it is afforded by the enforced reductions in the seasons 1883–84 and 1884–85. The extent of the falling back is unprecedented in the history of the industry, except during the cotton famine occasioned by the American war.[15]

By 1885 the Manchester Chamber of Commerce was convinced

that the best solution to this demand shortfall was the doctrinaire free-trade one of opening new outlets in hitherto unexploited regions of the world. According to the President of the Manchester Chamber:

> The important course that can bring lasting relief to our trade is that of securing and maintaining those free markets we possess and of opening up new channels for the sale of our manufactures. This is now felt by all the industrial countries of Europe, and has naturally become a motive for that policy of expansion and of annexation of territory which must increase in every quarter of the globe, as other industrial countries extend their trade, and our attention, therefore, must be devoted to new fields whose trade is free from all restrictions and differential duties—such as India and Central Africa —where there will be a constantly increasing demand for our goods, and where our manufacturers will find themselves in the best position to meet the competition of the world.[16]

Although the opening of new markets was primarily a task for individual effort, Manchester businessmen began increasingly to feel that private enterprise might require a helping hand from the state: 'The opening up of new markets, and the development of those already partially open to Great Britain,' the Manchester Chamber told the Royal Commission on the Depression of Trade and Industry in 1885, 'should be assisted by Government in every possible way'. These new markets were to be created, the directors believed, in Africa and Asia: '. . . openings now present themselves in Africa and by the encouragement of the scheme proposed by Mr A. R. Colquhoun for railway communication between British Burma and Western China . . .'.[17] These views were very common in business circles throughout Lancashire. Both S. Andrew, Secretary to the Oldham Master Cotton Spinners Association, and Joshua Rawlinson, Secretary of the North and North-East Lancashire Cotton Spinners and Manufacturers Association, in their replies to the Royal Commission on the Depression of Trade, stressed the necessity of increasing the effective demand for the products of the cotton industry by opening new markets in Africa.

The Association of U.K. Chambers of Commerce also urged the opening of hitherto unexploited regions of the world to British trade. A special committee of the Association concluded in 1885 that the economic condition of England, the growing population and increasing foreign competition made new markets an absolute necessity. It suggested that 'the fertile and populous countries between the Mediterranean and the Indus offer markets capable of considerable development',[18] but that any growth of trade in these regions required the construction of railways. Similarly, the countries lying to the north-east and south-east of India, Tibet, Burma, the Shan States, Siam and the Malay Peninsula were 'admitting of enormous development' if only adequate communications could be provided. The settlement colonies, the committee believed, were also important markets, especially in view of their high per capita consumption of British goods. It was essential therefore that measures be taken to direct the flow of British emigrants to the colonies.

While the empire of settlement attracted some attention in commercial circles in the mid 1880s, few British businessmen looked primarily to the settlement colonies for solutions to the country's economic problems. Their infrequent references to their colonial kinsmen overseas were more usually accompanied by expressions of regret over colonial tariffs than by panegyrics on the value of the imperial connection. Still there was hope in commercial circles that as the fool who persists in his folly may become wise, protectionist colonies like Canada and Victoria would eventually see the wisdom of returning to free trade.[19] During these years there was much talk of imperial federation in prominent British political circles, but most of it concentrated on the primary political decision-making process. An Imperial Parliament, a Grand Council of the Empire and the admission of colonial representatives to Westminster were all mooted in the 1880s. It was not, however, at this level that British businessmen considered the problem of inter-imperial relations in these years. Business attitudes towards the settlement colonies were concerned chiefly with inter-imperial co-operation at the most practical level. If not much could be accomplished in the sphere of fiscal policy, not to mention the thorny constitutional issues involved in schemes of imperial federation, there were other more mundane areas where commercial associations throughout the empire of settlement had common interests with their metropolitan counterparts. Agreement reached at the level of postage regulation, bankruptcy law and bills of lading could form a basis for the consideration of the larger fiscal and political issues.

Although mercantile collaboration over such matters in the mid 1880s did not produce any concrete schemes for an imperial commercial union, it generated a spirit of co-operation among businessmen throughout the Empire, leading—as we shall see later—to the Congress of Chambers of Commerce of the Empire in 1886. But few businessmen looked to the settlement colonies for a solution to the critical problem of over-production. It was to areas of the world 'hitherto neglected' or 'uncivilized' that businessmen looked for the new markets which they hoped would bring a revival of economic prosperity.

The Far East was one such area. What the advocates of an overland route from Burma to the Chinese interior failed to accomplish in the relatively prosperous 1870s was attempted with greater success in the depressed mid 1880s. Inspired by reports on the commercial potential of China by the explorer and publicist A. R. Colquhoun, British businessmen became seriously interested in the construction of an overland route to the Chinese interior from British possessions in Burma. In 1882 Colquhoun travelled from Canton to Yunnan, later visiting Burma, where he became convinced of the feasibility of an overland route from Martaban through the Shan States to Szumao. Arguing that the 'very grave depression of trade, the hostile tariffs enacted against our goods and the activity of our continental neighbours and rivals in competing abroad' made it necessary to 'discover new customers who are to be found in new markets',[20] Colquhoun appealed to commercial circles in Britain for support. It was hoped that the opening of communications with south-west China could be accomplished without government intervention and that chambers of commerce and other commercial groups in Britain would provide publicity and financial backing for the project.

The *Journal* of the London Chamber of Commerce readily took up Colquhoun's proposal and in 1883 became a leading proponent of a 'back door' into the allegedly rich market of south-west China. Emphasising the importance of opening new outlets to relieve over-production and the danger to British trade from French activities in Indo-China, it called for the early construction of a railway linking British possessions in Burma with the Chinese interior. The Council of the London Chamber of Commerce endorsed Colquhoun's appeal for subscriptions from London merchants towards the cost of a railway survey.[21] The explorer also received a warm welcome in Manchester, where he addressed a special meeting of the Manchester Chamber of Commerce on 21 December 1882. The President of the Manchester Chamber told the meeting that since the only way to balance supply and demand in the cotton trade was to open new overseas markets, Colquhoun's scheme was particularly worthy of support. The Manchester Chamber of Commerce subsequently sent out circulars to prominent Manchester businessmen endorsing the explorer's plan for a railway and his appeal for financial support.[22] The Glasgow Chamber of Commerce also agreed to help Colquhoun raise funds from its members.[23] Manchester subsequently contributed £393, while Glasgow and London raised £500 each. Colquhoun received contributions from other sources, including £500 from the Rangoon Chamber of Commerce, £300 from the Hong Kong Chamber and £100 from the Singapore Chamber. These enabled him to proceed with his survey in 1884–5.[24]

Meanwhile, relations between France and China steadily deteriorated over France's penetration of Tonkin.[25] Since the beginning of the 1880s China merchants and British officials had expressed fears that France aimed at the establishment of a preferential trading system in her possessions in Indo-China. Their anxieties increased after the outbreak of hostilities between France and China in August 1884. The British *chargé d'affaires* at Peking wrote to the Foreign Office the following May that 'it can hardly be doubted that the principle of protection will be applied by the French officials to the exclusion of British manufactures'.[26] These fears appeared to be justified by the Franco-Chinese treaty ending the hostilities signed at Tientsin on 9 June 1885. Commercial anxiety over the extension of French protectionism in Asia cast a dark shadow over the already gloomy economic situation and helped to transform mercantile support for the Colquhoun project into demands for a state-sponsored railway from British Burma to the south-west provinces of China.

Businessmen began to fear that private British enterprise in Asia would not be able to hold its own against the state-sponsored commercial activities of European rivals, especially at a time when competition was sharpened by severe demand shortages in traditional markets. A special meeting of the London Chamber of Commerce in April 1885 called upon the government to pay for the proposed Burma railway from the surplus funds of the Burmese

Administration.[27] The following month the Glasgow Chamber urged the British Government to guarantee the interest on the capital required for the construction of a railway between Burma and western China.[28] In July a delegation from the Manchester Chamber of Commerce interviewed Lord Randolph Churchill at the India Office and urged the early construction of a railway along the route suggested by Colquhoun.[29]

Though these mercantile requests for government action were all put forward on doctrinaire free-trade grounds, they in fact reflected a significant shift in business attitudes towards the government's responsibility for the state of the national economy. Because of their commitment to free trade, the only form of anti-cyclical policy acceptable in British mercantile circles was the extension of the world's free-trading area by opening new markets. Government assistance in this task was considered perfectly compatible with free-trade theory. But in the changed economic circumstances of the mid 1880s, conventional free-trade wisdom was leading businessmen to favour increased government intervention abroad.

It was in 1885 that commercial interest in a proposed overland route to China from Burma became linked in the British mercantile mind with the political future of the Kingdom of Burma. British merchants in Rangoon had been pressing the government to annex independent or Upper Burma since the beginning of the 1880s. By the middle of that decade they began to receive support from commercial circles in Britain on the grounds that political conditions in Upper Burma militated against the growth of British trade with the country and because Burma formed part of the 'highway to China'. Before examining mercantile attitudes towards Burma, however, it is necessary to glance briefly at the political situation in the Far East in the 1880s.

The Anglo-Burmese wars of 1823–6 and 1851–2 resulted in the cession to Britain of the Burmese provinces of Assam, Arakan, Tenasserim and Pegu, including the important port of Rangoon. Independent Burma was reduced to an inland kingdom oriented eastwards towards China and Siam. During the reign of the Burmese King Mindon Min, from 1852 to 1878, French activity in south-east Asia steadily increased as France extended her control from the original Colony of Cochin China to Annam and Tonkin. The extension of their influence into Laos brought the French into contact with the Shan States tributary to Burma. By the early 1880s, Upper Burma became a cockpit of Anglo-French rivalry in the Far East.[30]

When Mindon was succeeded by King Thibaw in 1878, Anglo-Burmese relations, which had begun to deteriorate towards the end of Mindon's reign, took a distinct turn for the worse. The new king fell under the influence of a palace clique which began to eliminate its political opponents by wholesale arrests and executions. Meanwhile, social disorder and gang robbery spread throughout the countryside as local administrative units broke down and revenue collection became difficult. With his influence at Mandalay rapidly waning, the British Resident and his staff withdrew to Rangoon and regular diplomatic relations between Britain and Upper Burma virtually ceased.[31]

The British business community in Rangoon had long advocated more active British intervention in Upper Burma. The merchants chafed under restrictions imposed on trade by the Burmese Government; they regarded Upper Burma as a potentially valuable market for British manufactures and they wished to obtain unimpeded access to Upper Burma's forest and mineral resources. Strong pressure was put on the British Government for the return of the Resident to Mandalay with a sufficient armed force at his disposal to ensure his security. The unrest in Upper Burma in the 1880s and alarming reports of French diplomatic activity at Mandalay led Rangoon businessmen to demand the annexation of Upper Burma. Annexation alone, the merchants argued, would put an end to the disorder, secure the country permanently against the French and open up Burma's resources of oil, timber and minerals. Individually and through the Rangoon Chamber of Commerce the merchants attempted to enlist the backing of commercial opinion in the metropolis for intervention in Thibaw's Kingdom.[32]

Their efforts were largely successful. At the beginning of 1885 Walter D. Dick of Messrs James Findlay and Company and John Galloway of the Irrawaddy Flotilla Company, both prominent Glasgow merchants, complained to the directors of the Glasgow Chamber of Commerce of the serious economic consequences of the unrest in Upper Burma. They alleged that the 'serious and continuing depression in the Burma trade was due directly to the unsettled state of the country'.[33] The Glasgow Chamber of Commerce subsequently submitted a memorial to the government urging the return of the British Resident to Mandalay accompanied by an armed guard.

Towards the end of 1885, after alarming rumours of an intensification of French diplomatic activity at Mandalay, Galloway again drew the attention of the Glasgow Chamber to Burmese affairs. At a special meeting of the Chamber's Foreign Affairs Committee in October 1885 several British merchants recently returned from Rangoon reported that feeling among the Burmese was overwhelmingly in favour of their country being placed under British rule. At the committee's request the Glasgow Chamber urged the Secretary of State for India 'to pursue such instant and effective measures as in their opinion may be best fitted for permanently securing the commercial interests of Great Britain in Upper Burma and the well being of its people'.[34]

Although the Glasgow merchants did not specifically urge a British take-over of Burma, there was no doubt that they welcomed that step when it came in January 1886. At the Annual Meeting of the Glasgow Chamber on 18 January, the President alluded to the rapid increase in the trade of British Burma since 1874; the same growth, he said, could now be expected from Upper Burma: 'By this annexation we may expect a great and continuously growing outlet for our manufactures'. Referring to the then-existing depression in trade and industry, Sir James Watson, a prominent director, told the Chamber that 'among the various causes and remedies proposed there was one with which they would all agree and that was the necessity of having new markets opened up for their commodities'. Little could be expected of Europe, or the United States, although there was still some hope for free trade in these areas in the future, 'but from the colonies, and especially the new Colony of Upper Burma, they might expect very much'.[35]

The London Chamber of Commerce displayed an even greater enthusiasm for the annexation of Upper Burma. In March 1885 London merchants in the Burma trade met at the offices of the London Chamber of Commerce. The meeting was presided over by E. Garnet Man, a former legal adviser to the British Government in Rangoon and an ardent exponent of the expansion of the British Empire. Man was the author of several works on the economic conditions of England and it was his concern with the problem of over-production that led him to advocate the expansion of the Empire. Believing that Britain's economic decline was the most serious issue of the day, Man's remedy was that 'emigration should be encouraged and annexations, if forced upon us, be carried out as opportunity occurs, for the trade of England follows the flag'.[36] The Burma merchants strongly urged the London Chamber of Commerce to press the British Government for the annexation of Burma. Although the Council of the London Chamber would not at first commit themselves to annexation, they were in favour of the intervention of the British Government to re-establish 'law and order' in Upper Burma. Uncertain as to how the British Government could intervene in Thibaw's kingdom, their memorial called for the return of the British Resident to Mandalay supported by a 'sufficient military force', and the immediate establishment of mixed courts to try cases involving both British and Burmese. At the meeting of the Chamber's deputation with Kimberley on 25 March, however, it appeared that many merchants, including S. S. Gladstone, who led the deputation, were openly in favour of annexation.[37]

This feeling gained ground during the summer of 1885. London merchants grew more and more in favour of annexation 'rather than the incomplete action of a Protectorate, which, it was feared, would encourage European intrigue'.[38] In July 1885 the Council of the London Chamber of Commerce took up the cry of the Rangoon merchants that until the annexation of Thibaw's domains 'nothing can be done to develop their natural resources and convert them into rich markets for British products and manufactures'.[39] British commercial ascendancy in eastern Asia was essential, argued the London Chamber's *Journal* in October 1885, for 'there can be no question whatever as to the necessity of new markets as affording relief to our present depressed trade'.[40] In November the London Chamber advocated the annexation of Upper Burma and the extension of British protection to the Shan States and Siam because 'the only attainable means of promoting a general rise in prices lies in the development of our trade with semi-civilized countries'. Europe was becoming yearly less valuable as a market, the London merchants believed, and 'England can only continue to live and prosper industrially by a spirited and far-seeing development of her colonial empire'.[41]

After complaints by its East India and China Trade Section, the Liverpool Chamber of Commerce urged the British Government to take immediate steps to protect British trade with Burma.

Robert S. Gladstone, a prominent East India merchant and Chairman of the Chamber's East India and China Trade Section, informed the government that the Liverpool merchants had no wish to suggest particular measures for the restoration of order in Burma. However, after British forces defeated the army of the King of Burma in November 1885, the Liverpool Chamber began to call for the annexation of Thibaw's kingdom. Such a step would, in the opinion of the Liverpool merchants, be 'a great advantage to the trade of England' and to the welfare of the people of Burma. Liverpool businessmen had no desire for an aggressive foreign policy but 'when they found that British trade was suffering abroad, and it was found necessary to annex a semi-barbarous country, it was better to do it and let it be known that the act is final'. The annexation of Burma, in their estimation, 'had opened up a valuable market, and if our foreign policy was firm it would have valuable influence on the restoration of commercial prosperity'.[42]

The directors of the Manchester Chamber of Commerce were approached several times during 1885 by other British chambers of commerce and by individuals involved in the Burma trade but they assiduously refused to support British intervention in the affairs of Upper Burma on doctrinaire free-trade grounds. Paradoxically, the same free-trade arguments were used by the Manchester merchants to justify the annexation of Upper Burma once that step had been taken. As the President of the Manchester Chamber pointed out in February 1886, the annexation put a stop to obstructions to British trade in a region of considerable economic potential.[43]

There can be no doubt that the government's decision to annex Upper Burma in 1886 was strongly influenced by pressure from commercial circles in Britain. The Liberals, who had authorised the military campaign that led to the defeat of Thibaw, claimed with typical Gladstonian sophistry that Upper Burma was annexed to 'protect' the frontiers of India. But this was simply a convenient way of permitting the government to charge the cost of the Burma campaign to the Government of India, thereby relieving the British taxpayer of the burden of empire. The real reason for the take-over of Upper Burma was economic. As the Conservative Lord Salisbury admitted with more candour in the House of Lords after his Administration had decided to annex the country, 'annexation of Burma had opened up a large and prosperous trade with those vast districts of China which hitherto we have been unable to reach'.[44]

Notes

1 *MBCC*, 4 April 1883.
2 Allen, *Industrial Development of Birmingham*, pp. 218–20.
3 See below.
4 *Annual Meeting of the Glasgow Chamber of Commerce* (hereafter *AMGC*), 9 Jan. 1882.
5 See C. Gertzel, 'John Holt: A British Merchant in West Africa in the Era of Imperialism', Ph.D. thesis, Oxford, 1959.
6 See P. N. Davies, 'Sir Alfred Lewis Jones and the Development of West African Trade', M.A. thesis, Liverpool, 1963.
7 *Chamber of Commerce Journal* (hereafter *CCJ*), 1 Nov. 1882.
8 *CCJ*, 5 May 1884.
9 *CCJ*, 5 June 1884.
10 Calculated from Hoffman, *British Industry*, Table 54, Part B, cols. 28, 29.
11 Ellison, *Cotton Trade*, pp. 297–301.
12 See *MG*, 6 Aug. 1882; 7 Dec. 1883; 6 May 1884. Also *The Economist*, Monthly Trade Supplement, 12 Jan. 1884.
13 *PMCC*, 19 Feb. 1879.
14 *The Economist*, 21 Feb. 1885.
15 Ellison, *Cotton Trade*, pp. 304–5.
16 *MG*, 3 Feb. 1885.
17 *Royal Commission on the Depression of Trade and Industry* (Appendix A), *Parliamentary Papers*, 1886, XXI, Reply of the directors of the Manchester Chamber of Commerce.
18 *RACC*, Feb. 1885.
19 See, for examples, *MLCC*, 9 Nov. 1883. *LDC*, 10 Dec. 1883. *AMGC*, 14 Jan. 1884.
20 *CCJ*, Supp., 5 Nov. 1887.
21 See *CCJ*, 5 Feb. 1883; 5 June 1883. *Report of the London Chamber of Commerce* (hereafter *LCCR*), 1883.
22 *MG*, 13 Dec. 1882; 6 Feb. 1883.
23 *MGCC*, 5 Nov. 1882; 11 Dec. 1882; 8 Jan. 1883; 12 Feb. 1883.
24 *CCJ*, Supp., 5 Nov. 1887.
25 See Lloyd Eastman, *Throne and Mandarins. China's Search for a Policy during the Sino-French Controversy 1880–85*, Cambridge, Mass., 1967, pp. 30–60.
26 Quoted from E. V. G. Kiernan, *British Diplomacy in China, 1880–85*, New York, 1970, pp. 125–44.

[27] *CCJ*, 5 May 1885.
[28] *MGCC*, 27 May 1885.
[29] *PMCC*, 29 July 1885.
[30] See John F. Cady, *A History of Modern Burma*, New York, 1958, pp. 67–110, and Woodman, *Making of Burma*, pp. 154–214.
[31] For an assessment of these events from the point of view of a modern Burmese scholar, see Maung Htin Aug, *The Stricken Peacock: Anglo-Burmese Relations 1752–1948*, The Hague, 1965. See also Cady, *History of Modern Burma*.
[32] See D. P. Singhal, *The Annexation of Upper Burma*, Singapore, 1960, pp. 71ff. See also Cady, *History of Modern Burma*, pp. 112–120 and Woodman, *Making of Burma*, pp. 216–34.
[33] *Minutes of the Foreign Affairs Committee of the Glasgow Chamber of Commerce* (hereafter *GFAC*), 7 Jan. 1885; 20 Feb. 1885; 10 April 1885. *MGCC*, 13 Aug. 1885. *RGCC*, 1885.
[34] *MGCC*, 24 Oct. 1885.
[35] *AMGC*, 18 Jan. 1886.
[36] E. Garnet Man, *The Present Trade Crisis Critically Examined*, London, 1885, p. 46.
[37] *CCJ*, 10 March 1885; 4 April 1885. *LCCR*, 1885.
[38] *Ibid.*
[39] *CCJ*, 4 July 1885.
[40] *CCJ*, 5 Oct. 1885.
[41] *CCJ*, 5 Nov. 1885.
[42] *Minutes of the Council of the Liverpool Chamber of Commerce* (hereafter *MLCC*), 3 Dec. 1885. *LDC*, 4 March 1886.
[43] *PMCC*, 25 March 1885; 30 Sept. 1885; 28 Oct. 1885; 30 Dec. 1885. *MG*, 2 Feb. 1886.
[44] *Parliamentary Debates*, 3rd ser., vol. 302, p. 60, cited in Singhal, *The Annexation of Upper Burma*, p. 85. See also Churchill's letters to Dufferin in Sept., Oct. and Nov. 1885, cited in R. J. Moore, *Liberalism and Indian Politics, 1872–1922*, London, 1966, p. 48.

Five

The imperialism of free trade: Africa in the mid 1880s

Many businessmen at first thought that free trade in Africa might be pursued without the interference of governments. As in the case of Burma, however, free trade in Africa in the 1880s seemed to require ever greater degrees of state intervention. The severity of the economic recession, together with the difficulties of opening up 'undeveloped' regions and keeping them out of the hands of protectionist rivals, appeared to demand the active assistance of the British Government. International guarantees of free trade, diplomacy to keep out foreign rivals, charters and concessions to attract the capital needed for development were all tried and found wanting. Before the end of the 1880s British businessmen were driven to the conclusion that in the final analysis free trade in Africa would be safeguarded only under some form of British protectorate or colony.

This imperialism of free trade reflected the basic economic motivation of late nineteenth-century expansionism. Commercial interest in Africa in the mid 1880s stemmed essentially from the recession in trade and industry and its intensity varied according to the extent different economic groups were affected by the slump. That Manchester was the most enthusiastic advocate of new African markets was hardly surprising, since the cotton trade was hit hardest of all by the recession.

One of the regions that attracted the most attention in commercial circles in the mid 1880s was the basin of the Congo River. The Congo appeared to provide relatively easy commercial access to one of the potentially richest markets on the African continent. If Britain was to benefit economically from the opening of the Congo to European commerce, there would have to be some kind of assurance that free trade would prevail in that region. As protectionism steadily gained ground in Europe and the continental powers began to turn their attention towards Africa, there was a growing danger that European protectionists would attempt to carve out exclusive commercial spheres in the 'Dark Continent'. The state would have to come to the assistance of free trade in Africa.

It was largely because of these dangers that the British Government began negotiations with Portugal towards the end of 1882 for the recognition of Portuguese territorial claims on the Congo. The activities of Leopold, King of the Belgians, on the Upper Congo and the rival operations of Savorgnan de Brazza, the agent of a group of French African enthusiasts, stirred the Portuguese into a reassertion of their centuries-old claim to the territory between 5° 12′ and 8° south latitude on the coast of Africa. Portugal's claim to this territory, which would give her control over the mouth of the Congo River, had been consistently denied by successive British governments since the time of Lord Palmerston. The British Foreign Office was prepared to reconsider this attitude in 1882 largely because of fear lest French recognition of treaties which de Brazza had made with chiefs on the Upper Congo lead to an extension of French protectionism in Africa. Although Gladstone's government regarded such an eventuality as a serious threat to British trade with south-west Africa, it was not prepared in 1882 to advance Britain's own territorial claims to that region. The Foreign Office proposed to rely instead on a less overt method to protect British interests. Portugal would be installed on the Congo in order to keep other potential candidates out. Since the Portuguese could be expected to prove amenable to British diplomatic pressure, this happy solution would preserve British commercial preponderance on the Lower Congo without directly involving the British Government.[1]

While this solution to the problem of preserving free trade on the Congo might appeal to British diplomats, it turned out to be anathema to British businessmen. The notion of installing Portugal on the Congo produced an uproar in the commercial community in Britain. Portugal was regarded by British businessmen as one of the most reactionary countries in Europe; her Catholicism and protectionism were heartily detested in Protestant free-trading Britain. British merchants soon made it clear that they would not

58

accept the nomination of such an unlikely candidate for the role of watchdog of free trade on the Congo.

When in June 1882 J. F. Hutton, the influential African merchant of Manchester, reported rumours to the effect that the Portuguese intended to establish a settlement at Nokki on the Congo, the Manchester Chamber of Commerce immediately protested to the British Government. They were reassured only when the Foreign Office privately showed John Slagg, the Manchester M.P., reports from Lisbon discounting any Portuguese intention of forcing their Congo claims by unilateral action.[2] The Foreign Office could not refer openly to the negotiations with Portugal, which actually began in November 1882, for these were not officially acknowledged by the government until February of the following year. However, rumours of the negotiations were fairly widespread. In November 1882 the Manchester Chamber of Commerce urged the government to appoint a consular agent to the Congo and to place a small steamer or gunboat at his disposal. Some of the directors feared that in view of possible official support for Stanley and de Brazza by the French and Belgian Governments, a consul and gunboat would be insufficient to protect British interests on the Congo. They did not, however, call for the assertion of British jurisdiction as a counter-measure. Instead, they favoured an international solution: the Manchester memorial to the Secretary of State included a suggestion that the British Government seek a 'friendly understanding' with other powers interested in the Congo. Additional force was given to these arguments by a deputation from the Manchester Chamber which met Dilke at the Foreign Office on 15 November.[3]

Strong mercantile opposition to the negotiations with Portugal began to materialise during November and December 1882. At first protests were confined to firms and individuals directly involved in the Congo trade. But the opposition soon took on more serious proportions. On 5 December 1882 the Liverpool Chamber of Commerce pointed out to the Foreign Office that de Brazza's treaty would exclude England 'from the prospect of any settlement being made by her traders on the Congo'.[4] Towards the end of the year, the directors of the Glasgow Chamber of Commerce urged the British Government to maintain 'the sovereign and territorial rights of the natives' and to preserve the neutrality of the Congo River.[5]

59

In the House of Commons Jacob Bright, one of the Manchester Liberal M.P.s, asked the government in November whether it could give any assurance that contemplated territorial changes on the Congo would not disturb freedom of trade between England and that part of Africa. Bright's question was put after consultation with the directors of the Manchester Chamber of Commerce, who were now determined to obtain definite assurance from the government that free trade on the Congo would continue undisturbed.[6] When, at the end of January 1883, the administration made a purely perfunctory reply to a further inquiry from the Manchester merchants, W. E. Foster, M.P. for Bradford, again raised the question of the Congo negotiations in the House. Receiving no assurance from the government's reply, the directors of the Manchester Chamber decided that stronger measures were required. The directors now resolved to mobilise commercial opinion throughout the country in preparation for a parliamentary campaign against the Anglo-Portuguese Congo negotiations. Bright agreed to lead the opposition to the negotiations in the House of Commons. The Manchester Chamber's correspondence with the Foreign Office was printed and copies sent to leading chambers of commerce requesting their 'prompt support' in denouncing any treaty with Portugal for the recognition of Portuguese jurisdiction on the Congo.[7]

One of Manchester's most outspoken opponents of the Anglo-Portuguese Congo negotiations was James F. Hutton. Throughout the winter of 1882 and the spring of 1883 Hutton was in correspondence with William Mackinnon, a prominent Glasgow businessman deeply involved in East Africa. Mackinnon was closely associated with Leopold, King of the Belgians, who was at the time building a chain of stations on the Upper Congo. Leopold had strong reasons for opposing any Anglo-Portuguese Congo agreement, which might threaten the future of his International Association by giving Portugal control over the mouth of the Congo. The Belgian king repeatedly pointed out this danger in personal letters to British officials and through influential Britons such as John Kirk and William Mackinnon, who wrote to the Foreign Office on his behalf. In the early stages of the opposition to the Anglo-Portuguese negotiations there was close co-operation between Leopold and prominent British opponents of a Congo treaty with Portugal.[8] British mercantile opposition to the negotiations was not engineered by Leopold, however, it was rooted in the merchants' determination to preserve free trade on the Congo, which was at the time most immediately threatened by the negotiations with Portugal. That this concern was widespread among British businessmen is clear not only from the vigour with which Manchester opposed the negotiations but also from the impressive opposition which developed in the other major commercial centres in 1883.

Although most of the mercantile opposition in the spring of 1883 was occasioned by Manchester's appeal for support, Manchester would not have been so successful were it not for the widespread belief in business circles that British trade and industry were suffering from an over-production of goods that could be most effectively relieved by opening new markets to absorb the excess supply of manufactures. In these circumstances any attempt to restrict access to a potentially valuable market was bound to encounter strong opposition from commercial opinion throughout the country. However, the government was hardly prepared for the massive commercial pressure that was brought against the Congo negotiations in the spring of 1883.

The prospect of the imposition of Portuguese—or indeed any—fiscal controls on the Congo was not encouraging for the Birmingham gun makers or the merchants who exported small arms to Africa, some of whom were represented in the Birmingham Chamber of Commerce. In response to Manchester's circular in March 1883, the Birmingham Chamber of Commerce urged the Foreign Office to obtain an international agreement 'so that in future there may be no interference on the part of any Power with the existing Free Trade and commerce of [the Congo] and its tributaries'.[9] Responding to Manchester's appeal for support in opposing the Congo negotiations with Portugal, the London Chamber of Commerce wrote to the Foreign Office pointing out that in view of the fact that the Congo promised to be a great future market for British manufactures, no foreign power should be permitted to establish claims that might later be used to impede freedom of trade and navigation. The London merchants suggested the establishment of a system of international regulations for the Congo. In April the *Chamber of Commerce Journal* drew attention to the dangers to free trade from Portuguese activities on the Congo and stressed the potential of that part of Africa as a market for manufactured goods.[10] During the early months of 1883 Liverpool merchants kept up a steady pressure on the British Government by writing letters to the Foreign Office individually and through the African Association, which organised a deputation of Liverpool merchants to the Foreign Office in February. E. Whitley, Conservative M.P. for Liverpool, took up the demands of the Liverpudlians in the House of Commons.[11]

In addition to protests from the major commercial and industrial centres, the Chambers of Commerce of Bristol, Cardiff, Dewsbury, Greenock, Huddersfield, Sunderland and Warrington made representations against the Congo negotiations to the Foreign Office in the spring of 1883.[12] Meanwhile, the directors of the Manchester Chamber of Commerce prepared the ground for parliamentary action against the negotiations by an extensive lobbying of M.P.s and chambers of commerce.

By 4 April, when Bright tabled his motion in the House of Commons deprecating any agreement with Portugal which would interfere with the *status quo* on the Congo, the agitation in the country had seriously alarmed the government. Speaking in the House of Commons, Bright reminded the government that commercial opinion in all the major centres was solidly opposed to the admission of Portugal to the Congo. The Prime Minister, in reply, promised that Parliament would be given an opportunity to consider any treaty with Portugal before it was submitted to the House for ratification.[13] The government agreed to this unprecedented step rather than risk defeat in the Commons, a very real possibility in the spring of 1883 despite its overall majority in the House.

The negotiations with Portugal, which continued throughout the remainder of 1883, showed that the British Government was constantly aware of mercantile objections to any treaty admitting Portuguese territorial claims on the Congo. This consideration was reinforced by an awareness on the part of key Foreign Office officials of the potential value of the Congo as a future market for Britain.[14] The Treaty with Portugal, which was eventually signed in February 1884, was largely on British terms and clearly attempted to meet most of the commercial objections made in the spring of 1883. Its provisions included a rigorous definition of freedom of trade and navigation on the Congo, to be protected by an international commission; the Mozambique tariff of 1877 was to be fixed as the maximum duty for ten years, after which tariff changes could be made only by mutual consent of the contracting parties; and there were explicit guarantees that British ships and goods would in all respects be on the same footing as the ships and goods of Portugal.[15]

Despite these modifications, the Manchester merchants refused to accept the treaty. It was argued by Hutton and other African merchants that under the Mozambique tariff of 1877 the duties on most Manchester exports to the Congo would be assessed at 25 to 35 per cent of their value. This, they declared, would seriously injure the trade of Manchester at a time when every possible market was needed. At a meeting of the Chamber's Committee on Congo Affairs on 5 March 1884, the directors decided to oppose the treaty *in toto*. They resolved to send circulars to chambers of commerce and M.P.s throughout the country urging them to oppose the ratification of the treaty.[16]

During March and April 1884, commercial opinion throughout Britain came out strongly against ratification of the Anglo-Portuguese Congo Treaty. As in the previous year, this was largely because of the recession, whose increasing severity in 1884 brought a deepening of commercial pessimism. The Manchester circular opposing ratification of the Congo Treaty with Portugal stressed the fact that under the Mozambique tariff the duties on Birmingham goods would be as high as 120 per cent of their value. Under the terms of the treaty guns were to pay a specific duty of 6s. 8d. each. Since this was the approximate cost of an African musket f.o.b. at Liverpool, the duty amounted to 100 per cent. The Birmingham arms manufacturers, already suffering from the combined effects of the recession and severe Belgian competition in the market for African muskets, were vehemently opposed to the Congo Treaty. These and other Birmingham merchants opposed to the treaty made their opposition known through the Birmingham Chamber of Commerce.[17] The Glasgow Chamber of Commerce opposed the Anglo-Portuguese Congo Treaty because they felt the British Government had made a bad bargain. British goods might be excluded from a potentially valuable market because of an ambiguous and possibly discriminatory tariff.[18] The leading African merchants in London were so vehemently opposed to the Congo Treaty that they organised themselves in a pressure group which became the basis of the London Chamber of Commerce West African Trade Section. Meanwhile the London Chamber sent a deputation to the Foreign Office to oppose the treaty.[19] In Liverpool, the Chamber of Commerce petitioned the Commons against the Anglo-Portuguese Congo Treaty on the grounds that its provisions for safeguarding free trade were worthless. The treaty was also opposed by the Liverpool African Association and a new organisation—the Congo District Defence Association—which came into existence in May 1884. Membership in this body was not restricted to Liverpool; the organisation included the larger British merchants and shipowners involved in the Congo trade, many of whom stood to lose personally by an extension of French or Portuguese jurisdiction to the river.[20]

In addition to protests from the major commercial and industrial centres the Chambers of Commerce of Bristol, Dewsbury, Halifax, Hull, Morley, Sheffield, Swansea and Wolverhampton also protested against the treaty with Portugal, many of them during March and April 1884. As in the previous spring, missionary and humanitarian bodies supported the commercial opposition.[21]

During March the Foreign Office attempted to meet the demands of its mercantile critics by pressing the Portuguese for further tariff concessions. The British Ambassador in Lisbon was instructed to ask for a guarantee that the duties on textiles would not be higher than 10 per cent. The Lisbon authorities were reluctant to grant this because of strong pressure from Portuguese manufacturing interests. But in return for a promise of British assistance in obtaining recognition of the treaty by the powers, Lisbon agreed to give the assurance desired. The government also attempted to persuade Manchester and Glasgow to drop their opposition to the treaty in return for reductions in the Portuguese tariff. However, most merchants refused to discuss the details of the tariff at all and demanded the total rejection of the treaty on the grounds that it was opposed to the principles of free trade.[22]

By mid April commercial opposition to the treaty, particularly in Lancashire, reached such proportions that the government began to have second thoughts about submitting it to Parliament. There was good reason for this, since the government was in a weak political position. The Liberal Party in 1884 was a house divided against itself, for despite a majority in the House of Commons, the Ministry could never be certain that a Whig–Radical split would not occur in the Commons. Moreover, the Liberals had no solutions for the growing economic and social problems of the eighties, which made them extremely vulnerable to Conservative attack. Conservatives were quick to capitalise on the economic distress in Lancashire in the spring of 1884 and to exploit the government's embarrassment over the Treaty with Portugal. The Conservative Leader, Lord Salisbury, visited Manchester in mid April and at a great Conservative demonstration in the Free Trade Hall, accused the government of contributing to the trade recession by irresponsible policies at home and by its failure to counter the spread of hostile foreign tariffs abroad:

> You know how the industry of this town has been cramped and fettered and confined by the growing wall of hostile tariffs which shuts you out of the markets of the world. I . . . don't know if that evil can be retarded, but at all events you must consider this—that if you are being shut out by tariffs from the civilized markets of the world, the uncivilized markets are becoming more and more precious to you; and they threaten to be the only field which will offer the most profitable business; and as civilization goes on, as exportation increases, these uncivilized markets will be thrown open to you, if only no foreign power is allowed to come in and interpose its hostile tariffs between you and the benefit for which you look.[23]

A few days after this, the African Committee of the Manchester Chamber of Commerce met Jacob Bright and a number of Liverpool merchants and steamship owners to discuss tactics for opposing the treaty in Parliament. After first considering the possibility of a debate in the House of Lords, the merchants decided to concentrate their efforts in the Commons. Plans were made to organise a mammoth deputation to the Prime Minister of representatives from Liverpool, Glasgow, Manchester, Birmingham and Sheffield to request the fixing of a date for discussion of the treaty in Parliament.[24]

By this time the opposition throughout the country had reached such proportions that the government was afraid to submit the treaty to the Commons. On 23 April the Parliamentary Under-Secretary at the Foreign Office advised that ratification be postponed or the government would certainly be beaten in the Commons. This 'would be serious in the present condition of affairs and very serious at Manchester from the party point of view'.[25] The Ministry, accepting this assessment, decided not to submit the treaty to Parliament. Portugal was informed that before proceeding with ratification the government would assist her to obtain the assent of the other powers to the treaty.[26]

This was a vain hope, for in June 1884 Bismarck let it be known that the Germans were dead against the treaty. Although it was the Iron Chancellor's refusal that finally killed the Anglo-Portuguese Congo Treaty, the issue was really decided by the commercial opposition in Britain in March and April 1884. While the British campaign against the treaty was not restricted to commercial circles, the mercantile agitation was the primary factor in persuading the government to drop ratification. The objections of the merchants for the most part preceded those of the non-commercial interest groups, most of whose protests were received after the government's decision not to submit the treaty to Parliament.

It was largely because of the failure of the Anglo-Portuguese Congo Treaty that British merchants turned to the idea of an international solution to the problem of preserving free trade on the Congo. On 22 April 1884 Leopold, King of the Belgians, secured United States recognition of his International Association as a sovereign power. The American Government's sentimental attachment to the Republic of Liberia and its belief that the Association aimed at the establishment of similar free states on the Upper Congo helped Leopold to overcome the United States' traditional reluctance to become involved in foreign affairs. If Leopold's handling of the negotiations with France, leading to that country's recognition of the International Association on 23 April 1884, revealed the king's consummate skill as a diplomat, they also suggest an unscrupulous side to his character. In the agreement of 23 April, Leopold promised France first refusal of the International Association's territories should the latter ever be obliged to part with them. The French Government regarded the operation of this 'pre-emption' clause as simply a matter of time, a belief shared by many of the powers when the agreement later became known. Leopold, on the other hand, had no intention of ever permitting foreclosure to take place.[27]

The 'pre-emption' clause had an unforeseen consequence. Since commercial circles in Britain were unaware of Leopold's real intentions, his agreement with France was the Association's greatest liability in its attempt to secure British support. The 'pre-emption' clause was not, however, the only problem for Leopold. If

British businessmen were worried lest the Association's territories fall to protectionist France, there was also considerable doubt about the extent to which the Association itself was committed to free trade. Despite the free-trade mantle in which it cast itself, the Association's agents had concluded a number of exclusive treaties with chiefs on the Congo. Rumours of these agreements reached the English Press and the Foreign Office, where they had the effect of greatly weakening the Association's credibility.[28] Leopold's supporters made a strong bid to win the backing of British commercial opinion but apart from the Manchester Chamber of Commerce little help was forthcoming.

For a time it appeared that Leopold might win the support of the Association of U.K. Chambers of Commerce. The attractiveness of the Belgian monarch's offer was greatly enhanced by the eloquence of H. M. Stanley, who addressed the Association at the end of September. Stanley denounced the British Government's inactivity in Africa at a time when, according to the explorer, that continent was the scene of a struggle similar to the contest for the mastery of North America in the seventeenth and eighteenth centuries. In the Congo, Stanley emphasised, British manufacturers had within their grasp an extremely rich market. If the British Government was not willing to take the region under its protection, the International Association was prepared to develop the area on its own under a regime of free trade.[29]

Stanley's picture of the vast potential of Central Africa as a market for manufactured goods had a strong appeal to many in his audience and he might have won the Association's endorsement but for his open avowal of Leopold's reversion agreement with the French. It may have been that Leopold and his supporters considered it wiser to acknowledge the reversion agreement publicly; this might prevent it being used against them by their opponents. If this was what they expected, they must have been disappointed, for it was the reversion agreement that really destroyed Leopold's chances of support in British business circles, and in the end the Association of U.K. Chambers refused to endorse the explorer's proposals.[30] This had considerable influence in business circles throughout the country and the adverse publicity given to the reversion agreement almost cost Leopold the support of his Manchester allies. While British commercial opinion would have been satisfied with some form of international control that would provide guarantees for free trade on the Congo, there was little support for the idea of entrusting this task to Leopold's International Association. During the second half of 1884 commercial opinion in Britain was more concerned with Germany's annexations in West Africa than with events on the Congo. Bismarck's African acquisitions not only caused great alarm among West African merchants in Britain; there was widespread concern in commercial circles throughout the country. This mercantile interest was in contrast to the attitude of the Gladstone government, which appeared to be relatively undisturbed by Germany's entry into the colonial field.[31] Since it was widely believed that Bismarck had been indifferent to overseas expansion, Germany's territorial gains in the Cameroons and the Gulf of Guinea in 1884 came as a shock to British businessmen. There was great uncertainty as to the nature and extent of Germany's colonial aspirations and it was feared in British business circles that the Reich's West African acquisitions were the prelude to a policy of far-reaching overseas expansion. Whatever Bismarck's real motives for acquiring colonies,[32] there was little doubt about his intentions among British merchants, manufacturers and shipowners; they were convinced that Bismarck was about to set up an exclusive colonial regime for the benefit of German trade and industry. They felt certain that the Reich would shortly establish differential duties and subsidies to German shipping lines in West Africa. Worse still, this new German policy would be initiated in an area where there was a preponderance of British trade.

These British fears proved to be very much exaggerated. It appeared at an early stage in the Berlin West Africa Conference that the economic interests of Britain and Germany in West Africa were virtually identical, although before the situation was clarified by the definition of Germany's position on free trade in her African possessions, there was a sharp outcry from commercial circles in Britain. Prominent British chambers of commerce complained bitterly to the Foreign Office that it was the objective of the Germans to cut British trade out of their newly acquired territories by means of differential duties and subsidised shipping lines. Despite these fears, few businessmen urged the extension of British territory as a counter-measure to the German threat. Instead they pressed the government to conclude treaties with Germany to protect British trade in the Reich's new West African possessions. Trade not territory was their main concern.[33]

This commercial alarm over German colonialism in West Africa was short-lived. It became apparent very early in the discussions of the Berlin West Africa Conference, which commenced on 15 November 1884, that both powers wished to extend the principle of free trade where possible in Africa, in opposition to France and Portugal, who hoped to restrict its application if they could not exclude it altogether. As the conference progressed Britain and Germany drew closer together, for their agreement on free trade meant that they found themselves agreeing essentially on most other issues raised by the conference.[34]

On the question of the Congo, Germany originally proposed that the Berlin West Africa Conference prohibit all import duties in the Congo basin; France, backed by Portugal, protested vehemently against any such absolute prohibition. A compromise was eventually reached on a proposal by the Hamburg merchant Adolph Woermann, who attended the Conference as unofficial adviser to the German delegation, and the powers agreed to limit the ban on import duties to a period of twenty years.[35] Although Britain agreed to accept this twenty-year clause, the concession was resented in commercial circles, particularly in Lancashire. The Manchester Chamber of Commerce wrote a strong protest to the Foreign Office on 20 November, urging that the twenty-year limit be removed. Two weeks later the Oldham Chamber of Commerce voiced a similar request.[36] Oldham suffered severely from recession and industrial unrest in the winter of 1884–5 and the Oldham Chamber shared Manchester's conviction that relief could be obtained by stimulating demand through the development of new export markets. The Foreign Office informed the Oldham merchants that they had no reason to worry about the future of free trade in Africa; the British Government understood the twenty-year clause to mean that imports on the Congo would remain free of taxation for an indefinite period unless at the end of twenty years the powers unanimously agreed to the imposition of import controls.[37]

Despite this reply, officials in the Foreign Office were uncertain as to the meaning the other Powers attached to the twenty-year clause. When it became clear to British officials that France expected the prohibition against import duties to cease after twenty years, the Foreign Office was alarmed lest its reply to the Oldham merchants appear to place the government in a false position.[38] In January reports from the Berlin correspondent of the *Manchester Guardian* gave the impression that the whole free-trade settlement at Berlin was secure for only twenty years. At the same time rumblings of discontent began to come from commercial circles in Manchester, where James F. Hutton wrote letters to the Press strongly condemning the twenty-year clause.[39] The Foreign Office, fearing an outcry from the business community, was now extremely anxious to clear up the matter of the import duties before Parliament met.[40]

The distress in the cotton-manufacturing districts in the winter of 1884–5 would have provided highly inflammable material for a parliamentary attack on any governmental decision that appeared to surrender foreign markets to Britain's commercial rivals. The government was acutely aware of this and took steps to present the twenty-year clause in a more favourable light. A high official in the Foreign Office, Percy Anderson, prepared a despatch for the British Ambassador to send home from Berlin, presenting the British interpretation of the twenty-year clause. This was to be done even though the British were still uncertain about the interpretations of the other powers. The Ambassador's despatch was to be sent to the President of the Oldham Chamber of Commerce and published in leading provincial newspapers. At the same time the Ambassador was instructed to clear up the matter of the import duties at the conference.[41] Although the powers finally agreed that the prohibition against import duties on the Congo would run for only twenty years, this was not clear until the conference protocols were drawn up. The British Government was not disposed to open up the question again, now that its version had been presented to the commercial public in Britain. With everyone apparently satisfied at the time, the matter was allowed to drop.[42]

The Foreign Office's handling of the Congo duties question showed the government's extreme sensitivity to commercial opinion. When it proved impossible to secure an absolute prohibition of import duties on the Congo, the Foreign Office accepted the twenty-year limit but took advantage of confusion over the twenty-year clause to present its own more liberal interpretation to the business community at home.

Although territorial questions were expressly excluded from the Berlin Conference, several important African boundaries were settled in a series of negotiations which ran parallel to and were closely connected with the proceedings of the powers assembled at Berlin. Shortly after the Conference was announced, merchants in the West African Section of the London Chamber of Commerce passed a resolution giving their qualified approval to some form of international control for the Niger River, provided that similar controls were extended to the other great rivers in Africa, including the Senegal, Congo and Ogowe. The resolution was never transmitted to the Foreign Office, however, for it was not accepted by the Council of the London Chamber,[43] which had never been very enthusiastic about the conference. Moreover, although direct evidence is lacking, it seems highly probable that George Goldie, the Chairman of the National African Company, used his influence in the London Chamber's Council to block any suggestion that might curtail his company's freedom of operation. On 1 November 1884, Goldie informed the Foreign Office that he had bought out the last French company on the Niger and that the National African Company was now the sole European firm on the River.[44] A few days later, the Chamber's *Journal* called for the 'firmest retention of the fullest British rights over those territories on the African coast which we have obtained through original exploration, trade development, and the preservation of peace'.[45] In particular it declared that control of the Niger should be British and not international; British occupation would be an advantage to all nations and would be the best way to preserve free trade. The Manchester Chamber of Commerce also opposed international control of the Niger. In this the influence of James F. Hutton, a director of the National African Company, was clearly evident. Hutton pointed out to the Manchester merchants that as the Niger was virtually British in everything but name, on no account should the interference of an international commission, let alone any other Power, be contemplated.[46]

The Manchester merchants gave considerable attention to territorial questions on the Congo. Between mid December 1884 and mid February 1885 the International Association was involved in separate negotiations with France and Portugal for the definition of their respective boundaries on the Congo. The Association sought the support of Britain and Germany in pressing its claim to jurisdiction over the entire length of the Lower as well as the Upper Congo.[47] In its attempt to obtain British support the International Association appealed to the Manchester Chamber of Commerce.

In view of that body's opposition to previous French and Portuguese attempts to get control of the Congo it was not surprising that the directors continued to oppose the pretensions of these two powers when the boundary discussions were taking place. Manchester's opposition to France and Portugal meant *inter alia* support for the International Association, to which the Chamber was already committed before the Berlin Conference began.

In November 1884 the International Association became extremely alarmed over rumours that France and Portugal planned to partition the Congo between them. The Association's agents addressed an urgent appeal to the directors of the Manchester Chamber of Commerce for help in pressing the British Government to resist the pretensions of France and Portugal. If admitted, the claims of these two powers would have entirely cut off the Association from independent access to the sea. The Manchester Chamber's African Committee angrily charged that 'the Foreign Office in failing to instruct Sir Edward Malet to adequately safeguard the interests of Great Britain in the Congo District, equally with those on the Niger, is imperilling the position of our traders. . . .'.[48]

The directors of the Manchester Chamber at first planned to send the entire African Committee, accompanied by the M.P.s Slagg, Houldsworth, Bright and Armitage, to the Foreign Office and they telegraphed to request an immediate interview. When the Foreign Office replied that the Foreign Secretary, Lord Granville, was absent from town but that the Parliamentary Under-Secretary would receive them, the Manchester merchants changed their plans. They were determined to make a direct representation to the Foreign Secretary and they resolved to send Hutton and Helm, the Chamber's Secretary, immediately to London. At the same time a telegram was despatched urgently requesting an interview with Lord Granville, who was then at his Walmer residence.[49]

Together with John Slagg, Hutton and Helm proceeded to an interview with the Under-Secretary at the Foreign Office, after which they met Lord Granville at Walmer. The Manchester representatives stressed the importance of defining the boundaries of the new Congo State while the conference at Berlin was still sitting. They also insisted that the International Association should receive both banks of the Congo to its mouth. Meanwhile the African Committee of the Manchester Chamber of Commerce wrote to Adolph Woermann urging him to mobilise commercial opinion in Germany in support of the International Association.[50]

In conjunction with repeated direct representations to the British and German Governments by agents of the International Association, Manchester's efforts helped to determine the shape of the Congo boundary. The British Government, in co-operation with Germany, attempted to persuade the French to conclude a generous territorial settlement with the International Association. Although Bismarck refused the British Government's request to put direct pressure on France, he did elicit from the latter an admission of the Association's right to territory on the Congo, which paved the way for the final settlement on 5 February 1885.

For the Manchester merchants Portugal was an even greater threat than France because of the former's impenitent protectionism and past inability to develop her African possessions economically. During the first two months of 1885 the directors kept steady pressure on the Foreign Office to oppose the concession to Portugal of any territory on the Congo.[51] As the negotiations between Portugal and the Association dragged on, the African Committee of the Manchester Chamber of Commerce took an even more uncompromising position than Leopold himself and insisted that Portugal be entirely excluded from the south as well as the north bank of the Congo. The agreements which the International Association eventually concluded with France and Portugal met most of its wishes and those of its British supporters: the Association secured both banks of the Congo with the exception of the left bank from Nokki to the sea, which went to Portugal, and a belt of territory on the right bank above Manyanga obtained by France. The Manchester merchants were not entirely satisfied with the final settlement and continued to insist that Portugal be entirely excluded from the south bank. On the whole, however, the territorial settlements on the Congo and the Niger were not of great importance to the British commercial public; of far greater significance for British merchants was the fact that the conference appeared to provide an international solution to the problem of preserving free trade in Africa.

Appearances in this case were deceptive. Although Britain and Germany agreed on the widest possible application of free trade in their African possessions, in practice there were many obstacles to the smooth functioning of this principle. Nowhere was this more apparent than in the Gulf of Guinea, where the German annexation of Togoland added fresh complications to an already complex system of differential tariff zones. British, French and German fiscal areas were interspersed along the West African coast between Cape St John and Lagos. In practice the tariffs of all three powers tended to operate differentially; against French and German spirits in the British zone and against British arms and cloth in the French and German zones. Moreover, since these zones were limited to the coastal fringe, in some cases extending only a few miles into the interior, the first power to penetrate the area behind its coastal enclave would be able to divert trade from the interior away from its neighbouring competitors.[52]

The Liverpool merchants at first hoped that on the basis of an earlier treaty the British Government would persuade the Germans to withdraw from points between the Gold Coast and Lagos. Neither the Foreign Office nor the Colonial Office were prepared to accept any previous British commitment on that part of the coast, however, although British officials were anxious to assist traders to obtain equality of treatment in the French and German zones. Having failed to persuade the Foreign Office to recognise earlier British claims, merchants in Liverpool and London urged the government to negotiate an exchange of territory which would end the trading difficulties between Lagos and the Gold Coast. The London Chamber of Commerce wrote to the Foreign Office towards the end of January 1885 that the trading problems on the west coast could be solved by bringing 'the whole of the West Coast of Africa between the Gold Coast and Lagos . . . under the protection of Great Britain by means of negotiations with the severally interested Governments, native and European'.[53] Two weeks later the Liverpool Chamber of Commerce addressed a similar appeal to the Foreign Office, urging the British Government to acquire the German West African territories by exchange and to extend British jurisdiction to parts of the coast between Lagos and the Gold Coast then unprotected by any European power.[54] These mercantile demands illustrate clearly how their concern with free trade was leading British merchants to call for imperial expansion. Territorial questions were still regarded as strictly subordinate to the requirements of commerce but merchants were beginning to advocate extensions of territory that they believed were necessary to the security or the stability of trade.

At first this mercantile pressure for partition of African territory was restricted to the coastlines of West Africa. But the merchants soon began to exert pressure for the extension of British jurisdiction to the hinterlands of West Africa as well. The main impetus in this came from Manchester and once again it reflected the severity of the recession in the cotton trade in the mid 1880s. Manchester merchants were interested in the West African colonies because, if properly developed, they appeared to offer a promising market for cotton goods. By the mid 1880s the Manchester Chamber of Commerce was convinced that the Gambia, Sierra Leone, the Gold Coast and the districts bordering on the Niger and Benue Rivers must receive much greater attention from the British Government if their commercial potential was to be properly developed.

This conviction made the Manchester directors highly receptive to complaints of government neglect by merchants in the West African trade. In 1885 British merchants in the Gambia trade complained to the Manchester Chamber of Commerce that they had lost roughly 25 per cent of their capital during the previous two or three years. The merchants blamed most of this on the colonial authorities who, they alleged, were not providing adequate protection for traders in the interior. The merchants were particularly upset because the government was in their opinion not sufficiently firm in dealing with local 'disturbances'. The Manchester Chamber of Commerce addressed a strong protest to the Colonial Office demanding that as long as the Gambia merchants were taxed by the colonial government, they had the right to expect adequate protection for their lives and property.[55] Similarly in the case of Sierra Leone, the Manchester Chamber of Commerce took up the complaints of British merchants, who clamoured for greater government support. In May 1885 the Chamber wrote to the Colonial Office endorsing the demands of the Sierra Leone merchants for government intervention to put an end to inter-tribal warfare beyond the Colony's boundaries.[56]

The Manchester merchants also pressed the British Government to intervene in the hinterland of the Gold Coast Colony. As early as November 1883, the Manchester Chamber sent delegates to the Colonial Office to urge greater government activity in that Colony. The delegation, consisting of prominent Manchester businessmen, complained of a decline in exports of Lancashire manufactures to the Gold Coast. They urged the government to assist the development of Gold Coast trade by railway construction and by establishing official relations with chiefs outside British jurisdiction, particularly in Ashanti, where they suggested the appointment of a British Resident.[57] In neither Sierra Leone nor the Gold Coast was the government prepared to extend British influence into the hinterlands; much less were they willing to sanction the use of force for such a purpose.[58] It was not until the late 1880s and early 1890s after mercantile interests mounted a massive campaign for intervention that they forced the hand of the British Government.[59]

In the Bights of Benin and Biafra the Manchester directors believed there was a need for the appointment of additional consular officials to keep pace with the increased importance of British trade in that region. They indignantly rejected the government's suggestion that the cost of these should be paid by the merchants and shipowners. British trade in West Africa, they declared, was a national interest and the cost of its protection ought to be met from imperial funds.[60]

Although the Niger delta had been proclaimed a British protectorate in 1884, a year later it was still without more than a 'paper' administration. In September 1885 the Manchester Chamber of Commerce complained to both the Foreign and Colonial Offices that 'the present defenceless state of the Country creates considerable anxiety in the minds of the mercantile and industrial communities of this country and retards the future development of trade'.[61] Manchester's protest was probably prompted by George Goldie, who was at that time attempting to put pressure on the Foreign Office to obtain a charter for his National African Company. It was certainly Goldie who drew the attention of the London Chamber to the government's inactivity on the Niger and Benue. In September 1885 Goldie warned the London merchants of the dangers to British trade on the Niger unless the government established an effective police force for the maintenance of 'law and order'. The Berlin Conference, he reminded them, would recognise only effective occupation. The London merchants had just been discussing the recent German action in Zanzibar, where the Sultan had been forced by Bismarck to recognise Germany's protectorate in East Africa. In these circumstances Goldie had little difficulty in persuading the merchants to adopt a resolution urging 'the immediate establishment of an adequate police force to overawe predatory tribes as well as to enforce decisions of the judicial officers'.[62] This was in line with the London Chamber's general policy of demanding increased government support in opening new markets for British exports, a theme given prominence by Goldie in pressing for the establishment of British authority in the Niger districts: 'With old-established markets closing to our manufactures, with India producing cotton fabrics not only for her own use but for export, it would be suicidal to abandon to a rival power the only great remaining undeveloped opening for British goods.'[63]

The Manchester and London Chambers of Commerce not only pressed the government to protect trading interests; they also demanded improved communications, administration and transport facilities in West Africa. Towards the end of 1884, for example, the Chambers of Commerce of London and Manchester requested the government to establish direct British-controlled telegraphic communication with the west coast of Africa. By memorial and deputation to the Colonial Office, the Manchester directors took up the cry of the West African merchants for greater representation in the legislative councils of the West African colonies and the construction of railways to open up the interior to trade.[64] By all these means they hoped to enlarge their markets and bring about improved economic conditions in the depressed districts of Lancashire.

It was urged in some unofficial circles in 1884–5 that Britain ought to respond to Germany's West African annexations by asserting her authority in East Africa. Many businessmen and officials were aware that Africa was in the process of being partitioned among the European Powers and they feared losing a large area which in time could be developed into a valuable market for manufactures. Britain, it was argued, should expand her influence in East Africa before it was too late.

In July 1884 H. H. Johnston, a young botanist on an expedition to Mount Kilimanjaro, wrote home in glowing terms of the rich mineral and agricultural resources of the East African highlands. Later in the year Frederick Holmwood, British Consul at Zanzibar, drew the attention of the Foreign Office to the commercial importance of the highland region of East Africa, a theme also stressed by explorer Joseph Thomson's report to the Royal Geographical Society in November 1884.[65] These reports were favourably received by Percy Anderson, Head of the Foreign Office's African Department, T. Villiers Lister, the Assistant Under-Secretary, and

Lord Edmund Fitzmaurice, the Parliamentary Under-Secretary.[66] The Foreign Secretary, Lord Granville, appeared to agree on the importance of not permitting Kilimanjaro to pass into the hands of any foreign power. The Cabinet eventually decided to act on a suggestion by Clement Hill, a clerk in the Foreign Office, that British interests on the East African mainland could best be secured by persuading the Sultan of Zanzibar to exert his authority there. British trade could then be protected by diplomatic pressure on the Sultan, who had in the past proved highly amenable to British wishes. However, this decision was made without the full knowledge of Gladstone and the Prime Minister's subsequent refusal to agree on the necessity for taking any action whatever in East Africa meant that the plan had to be abandoned. The British Government settled for a declaration by the Sultan that he would not part with any of his territories without British consent.[67]

However, the Sultan's declaration was of little use to Britain when, on 3 March 1885, Bismarck published his *Schutzbrief* placing under German protection the territories on the East African mainland acquired by the explorer Karl Peters. Since the British Government had declined to define the mainland possessions of the Sultan, it had little grounds for protest had the British even wished to object officially. In fact the government was no more disposed to protest than it had been in the previous year when Germany made her West African annexations.

The Foreign Office came under considerable mercantile pressure to secure something for Britain in East Africa before it was too late. Even before the publication of Bismarck's *Schutzbrief*, commercial interests in Britain were beginning to move. At the end of January 1885 Holmwood drew the attention of the Manchester Chamber of Commerce to the commercial possibilities of East Africa. Speaking to the members of the Chamber at the annual meeting a few days later, the President pointed out that the mainland possessions of the Sultan of Zanzibar might become one of Britain's most valuable markets in the future. He emphasised the importance of preventing this region, where British influence was already paramount and free trade obtained, from falling into the hands of any foreign power. At a meeting in March, the directors of the Manchester Chamber of Commerce asked the government to retain Holmwood on leave for an additional month so that he might provide information and advice about commercial prospects in East Africa.[68]

Holmwood's scheme, which was similar in many respects to the one he had advocated in Manchester in 1879, called for the construction of a railway line from the East African coast to Kilimanjaro. Such a line would open to commerce a region which the Consul described as the 'richest and most healthy in tropical Africa'. The highlands of East Africa could become a field for emigration and an important market for the cotton goods of Lancashire. Holmwood presented his plan as a solution to the depressed condition of British industry: 'The undertaking would be eminently a patriotic one, for it would materially conduce to a revival of our now depressed trade, and were it supported by our Chambers of Commerce, and by a sufficient number of influential members of our Legislature and of the mercantile community, its success would not be doubtful'.[69]

He was not disappointed with Manchester's response. The African Committee of the Manchester Chamber of Commerce recommended his plan to Lord Granville in April 1885.[70] Meanwhile Holmwood won the backing of a group of prominent businessmen and politicians, many of them from the Manchester area. Besides Hutton and Mackinnon, the members of this group included Lord Aberdare, Chairman of the National African Company and an ex-cabinet member, Baron P. M. de Rothchild, Henry Broadhurst, the trade union leader, Henry Lee, M.P. for Southampton, and the three Manchester M.P.s, Jacob Bright, William Houldsworth and John Slagg. The promoters planned to form a company called the British East African Association to administer the mainland possessions of the Sultan of Zanzibar; in return the Association would pay the Sultan a guaranteed annual revenue and grant him one founder's share in the proposed company.[71]

During the summer of 1885 this group kept up steady pressure on the Foreign Office. They sought official backing for negotiations with the Sultan and they wanted government help in keeping the Germans out of the territory of the proposed concession.[72] Their demands were backed by the Manchester Chamber of Commerce; on 15 July 1885 the Manchester directors wrote to Salisbury supporting Holmwood's plan for a railway from Tanga or an adjacent port to the country around Kilimanjaro. Such a project, they emphasised, would not receive the necessary financial support without a concession similar to that sought by Mackinnon in 1879.[73]

At Slagg's suggestion the directors sent a deputation to the Foreign Office a week later. In an interview with the Permanent Under-Secretary, Hutton and Slagg stressed the importance of government support in obtaining a concession from the Sultan.[74] At the quarterly meeting of the Manchester Chamber in August, the President informed the members that the proposed East African railway would eventually be extended to Lake Victoria Nyanza and would open up a vast market for British goods.[75] It was not the strategic value of a link between the east coast and the Sudan that interested the Manchester merchants, nor were they greatly concerned with the value of the East African coastline; although the directors urged the Foreign Office to prevent the coastline from falling into the hands of the Germans, they were chiefly concerned with free access to the interior, wherein, they believed, lay the region's main economic potential. The Manchester merchants hoped that whatever annexations might be made on the coast, the government would take steps to ensure free access to markets in the interior.

Although officials in the Foreign Office were favourably inclined towards the scheme of Mackinnon and his associates, neither Lord Granville nor Lord Salisbury, who succeeded the former as Foreign Secretary in June 1885 and became also Prime Minister, was prepared to risk offending Bismarck. In May 1885 Granville informed the German Chancellor of the proposals of the promoters and assured him that the British Government would not support any scheme that might conflict with German interests.[76] This did not mean, however, that Gladstone's government were indifferent to commercial interests in East Africa, for earlier in 1885 the Foreign Office informed the German Government that the Sultan of Zanzibar had been for many years under the 'direct influence' of Great Britain and Granville's approach to Bismarck in May was in line with earlier British suggestions for a delimitation of spheres of influence.[77] Lord Salisbury's position was essentially the same. The Conservative Prime Minister took it for granted that the only important British interest in East Africa was commercial and that so long as British merchants had equal access to the region the government need not become involved. Salisbury was prepared to support free trade by diplomatic action if necessary but only to the extent of preserving the independence of Zanzibar. Further than this the government would not go.

Some officials accused commercial interests of being lukewarm in their desire to develop East Africa. This was really somewhat disingenuous, for the Foreign Office was perfectly aware that because of the scale and nature of the project, the promoters could not raise the necessary capital without official support. If the government would not guarantee the undertaking, Mackinnon and his associates hoped at least for official support in obtaining a concession from the Sultan. But the Foreign Office refused to offer assistance beyond that provided to any British subject overseas. Since it was clear to businessmen by the middle of the 1880s that the economic development of areas like East Africa was beyond the resources of unaided private enterprise, this was the end of the matter. British businessmen were already beginning to draw the conclusion that free trade in Africa would not flourish without strong government support but it was not until the following decade that they were able to force the government to involve itself directly in East Africa.

In June 1885 the British and German Governments agreed to establish a joint commission, to which France was invited, to determine the boundaries of the Sultan of Zanzibar's mainland possessions. For the German colonial enthusiasts this announcement was the signal for a burst of treaty-making activity, this time at Witu, north of the British sphere.[78] These treaties were serious from the British point of view, for hitherto German territorial claims had not directly conflicted with established British interests. The Foreign Office now recognised the need for some strong counter-move. As Mackinnon's concession scheme was suspended pending the outcome of the delimitation commission's findings, the government considered recognising a concession obtained by H. H. Johnston in the region of Mount Kilimanjaro.

At the end of October 1885, Percy Anderson, the head of the Foreign Office's African Department, informed Johnston privately that the British representative on the delimitation commission would support the Kilimanjaro concession if it could be claimed that a British company was actually involved in the district. Since Johnston did not have sufficient capital, Anderson suggested that the concession be made over to James Hutton, who was in a position to find financial backing for the formation of a company. In making this proposal to Hutton, Johnston urged the former to secure the support of the Manchester Chamber of Commerce which would, he suggested, show the Germans the seriousness of

British intentions.[79] Hutton agreed to take over the Kilimanjaro concession and immediately began to make plans for the formation of a company. He also submitted Johnston's proposals to a confidential meeting of the African Committee of the Manchester Chamber of Commerce on 14 November. However, the committee felt that since the scheme 'related to matters coming within the scope of private enterprise', it should be left to the individual initiative of Hutton.[80] It was partly because of the absence of strong commercial pressure for the assertion of British claims in the region that Kilimanjaro passed to Germany in the delimitation settlement of October 1886. Had commercial opinion mobilised behind the Kilimanjaro scheme the outcome would perhaps have been different.

The Anglo-German delimitation of 1886 restricted the mainland possessions of Zanzibar to a strip of territory ten miles in depth from Tunghi Bay to Kipini. The hinterland was partitioned into British and German zones. For the British, commercial motives were uppermost: no one seriously considered at the time that the hinterland was necessary for control of the headwaters of the Nile; until 1897 no British Government believed that a prolonged occupation of Egypt would be necessary. The only possible strategic threat to British interests in the area was the establishment of a foreign naval power on the coast, but this was not taken seriously by the Admiralty. The strongest pressure for the extension of British influence into the East African interior in 1885–6 came from commercial interests, officials and members of the consular service, and the economic possibilities of the hinterland was the dominant argument used by these groups. That they did not secure all they wanted in the 1886 delimitation was hardly surprising in view of the German desire for territory in the same region. They did secure most of what they wanted—a potentially valuable field for British investment and emigration and a market for British manufactures. That few were actually prepared to invest their money in East Africa and that little trade and no emigration occurred in the region until the twentieth century likewise does not discount the importance of commercial motives in the 1886 Anglo-German partition agreement. Rather, the rapid evaporation of business interest in East Africa after 1886 serves to highlight the speculative economic motivation of the partition. By the last quarter of 1886 an economic recovery had set in, and with a revival of business activity there was a return of commercial confidence and a corresponding decline of mercantile interest in schemes for stimulating the economy by opening new export markets in far-away places like East Africa.

Notes

1 This paragraph is based on the following: R. Anstey, *Britain and the Congo in the Nineteenth Century*, Oxford, 1962, pp. 37–49, 100–2; James Duffy, *Portuguese Africa*, Cambridge, 1959, pp. 208–11; Ruth Slade, *King Leopold's Congo*, London, 1962, pp. 35–9.

2 *PMCC*, 7 June 1882. FO 84/1802 Manchester CC to Granville, minute by Anderson, 15 June 1882.

3 FO 84/1862, Hatton and Cookson to FO, 17 Nov. 1882. *PMCC*, 6 Nov. 1882. *MG*, 7 Nov. 1882. FO 84/1631, Manchester CC to FO, 13 Nov. 1882.

4 FO 403/14, Liverpool CC to FO, 5 Dec. 1882.

5 FO 403/14, Hamilton M.P. to FO, 30 Nov. 1882 and encl.

6 FO 403/14, Question by Bright in the Commons, 28 Nov. 1882. *PMCC*, 27 Nov. 1882.

7 FO 403/14, Answer to Question in the Commons, 26 Feb. 1883. *PMCC*, 28 Feb. 1883.

8 *Mackinnon Papers* (hereafter *MP*), Hutton to Mackinnon, 27 Feb. 1883; same to same, 1 March 1883. See also Anstey, *Britain and the Congo*, pp. 126–32, and Slade, *King Leopold's Congo*, p. 38. For some of Leopold's efforts to secure British support see FO 403/14, Mackinnon to FO 13 Dec. 1883; same to same, 19 March 1883; Lambert to Rosebery, 9 Feb. 1883.

9 See FO 403/37, J. Wilson Browne to Fitzmaurice, 29 March 1884. FO 403/15A, Birmingham CC to FO, 24 April 1883.

10 FO 403/14, London CC to FO, 13 March 1883. *CCJ*, 5 April 1883.

11 FO 403/14, Irvine & Co. to FO, 14 Feb. 1883; Hatton and Cookson to FO, 13 March 1883; same to same, 20 March 1883. FO/1804, British and African Steam Navigation Co. to FO, 17 March 1883.

12 These are filed in FO 84/1805.

13 *Hansard*, CCLXXLL, Comm. 1284–96.
14 FO 84/1806, official minutes on Serpa to d'Antas, 26 June 1883. FO 84/1805, minute by Lister on Consul Cohen to FO, 16 April 1883. See also Anstey, *Britain and the Congo*, pp. 142–4.
15 The text of the Treaty is reproduced in *PP*, 1884, LVI, 45.
16 *MG*, 8 March 1884.
17 *MBCC*, 2 April 1884; 9 April 1884. FO 403/37, J. Wilson Browne to Fitzmaurice, 29 March 1884; Birmingham Fair Trade Union to FO, 22 March 1884; Mr Fowler M.P. to FO, 29 March 1884.
18 *MGCC*, 10 March 1884, FO 403/37, Glasgow CC to FO, 26 March 1884; same to same, 15 April 1883.
19 *Minutes of the West African Trade Section of the London Chamber of Commerce* (hereafter *LWAS*), 31 March 1884; 7 May 1884.
20 *LDC*, 8 March 1884; 16 May 1884; 23 May 1884. *LJC* 27 March 1884. *MLCC*, 26 March 1884. FO 403/37, Congo District Defence Association to FO, 21 July 1884; 7 Aug. 1884; 17 Oct. 1884.
21 Filed in FO 403/38 and FO 84/1810.
22 See FO 403/37, FO to Petre (tel.), 21 March 1884; Petre to FO (tel.), 24 March 1884; same to same, 25 March 1884; FO to Petre, 26 March 1884; Petre to FO, 23 March 1884; same to same (tel.), 27 March 1884. See especially Granville to Petre (tel.), 26 March 1884; Manchester CC to FO, 26 June 1883; H. C. Calcraft to Lister, 29 March 1884.
23 *MG*, 17 April 1884.
24 *PMCC*, 18 April 1884.
25 FO 84/1810, minute by Fitzmaurice, 23 April 1884.
26 FO 403/38, FO to Petre, 23 April 1884.
27 See S. E. Crowe, *The Berlin West African Conference, 1884–85*, New York, 1942, pp. 81–2. Anstey, *Britain and the Congo*, p. 170.
28 FO 84/1809, memo. by Anderson, 2 March 1884. See also Anstey, *Britain and the Congo*, pp. 157–8.
29 FO 83/807, Report by C. M. Kennedy.
30 *Ibid*.
31 See J. E. Flint, *Sir George Goldie and the Making of Nigeria*, London, 1960, pp. 62–3; and Hargreaves, *Prelude . . .*, p. 322.
32 This is still a highly controversial subject. See M. E. Townsend, *Origins of Modern German Colonialism*, New York, 1921, and

84

The Rise and Fall of Germany's Colonial Empire, New York, 1930; A. J. P. Taylor, *Germany's First Bid for Colonies*, London, 1938; W. O. Aydelotte, *Bismarck and British Colonial Policy*, Philadelphia, 1937; Henry A. Turner, 'Bismarck's Imperialist Venture: Anti-British in Origin?' in P. Gifford and W. R. Louis (eds), *Britain and Germany in Africa. Imperial Rivalry and Colonial Rule*, London, 1967. Perhaps the best work to appear on this subject is Hans-Ulrich Wehler's, *Bismarck und der Imperialismus*, Cologne, 1969.

[33] See, for examples, *LDC*, 26 Aug. 1884; 25 Sept. 1884; 9 Oct. 1884. *LJC*, 21 Aug. 1884; 9 Oct. 1884. FO 84/1690, Liverpool CC to FO, 8 Oct. 1884. FO 403/47, Liverpool CC to FO, 12 Nov. 1884. *MGCC*, 13 Oct. 1884; 10 Nov. 1884. FO 403/47, Glasgow CC to FO, 10 Nov. 1884. *LWAS*, 7 Oct. 1884. FO 84/1691, London CC to FO, 22 Oct. 1884.

[34] See Crowe, *Berlin West African Conference*, pp. 105ff.

[35] *Ibid.*, pp. 116–17.

[36] FO 403/48, Manchester CC to FO, 12 Nov. 1884; Oldham CC to FO, 26 Dec. 1884.

[37] FO 403/48, FO to Oldham CC, 31 Dec. 1884.

[38] FO 84/1820, Minute by Lister on Malet to Granville, 17 Jan. 1885. FO 84/1819, Official minutes on Malet to Granville, 10 Jan. 1885.

[39] FO 84/1820, Anderson to Pauncefote (Private), 17 Jan. 1885. *MG*, 19 Jan. 1885.

[40] FO 84/1820, Anderson to Pauncefote (Private), 17 Jan. 1885.

[41] FO 84/1820, Anderson to Pauncefote, 31 Jan. 1885.

[42] See FO 403/1820, Official minutes on Malet to FO (tel.), 31 Jan. 1885.

[43] *LWAS*, 27 Oct. 1884; 2 Dec. 1884.

[44] FO 403/47, Goldie to FO, 1 Nov. 1884. See also Flint, *Sir George Goldie*, pp. 67–8.

[45] *CCJ*, 5 Nov. 1884.

[46] *MG*, 4 Nov. 1884. *PMCC*, 20 Oct. 1884.

[47] For a detailed account of these negotiations, see Crowe, *Berlin West African Conference*, pp. 157ff.

[48] *PMCC*, 11 Dec. 1884.

[49] *PMCC*, 12 Dec. 1884.

[50] *PMCC*, 12 Nov. 1884. FO 84/1817, Memo. by Granville, 15 Dec. 1884. See also Anstey, *Britain and the Congo*, p. 177.

[51] See, for examples, *PMCC*, 19 Jan. 1885; 28 Jan. 1885; 30 Jan. 1885; 9 Feb. 1885. FO 403/49, Manchester CC to FO, 19 Jan. 1885; 30 Jan. 1885; 9 Feb. 1885.

[52] See C. W. Newbury, *The Western Slave Coast and its Rulers: European Trade and Administration among the Yoruba and Adja-Speaking Peoples of Southwestern Nigeria, Southern Dahomey and Togo*, Oxford, 1961, ch. V.

[53] FO 84/1732, London CC to FO, 21 Feb. 1885.

[54] FO 84/1781, Liverpool CC to FO, 5 Feb. 1885.

[55] *PMCC*, 9 Sept. 1885. For details of the situation in the Colony of the Gambia around this time, see H. A. Gailey, *A History of the Gambia*, New York, 1965, pp. 39–60.

[56] *PMCC*, 20 May 1885; 25 May 1885. For details, see Christopher Fyfe, *A History of Sierre Leone*, Oxford, 1962, pp. 451–4.

[57] *PMCC*, 28 Nov. 1883. CO 96/154, Manchester CC to CO, 7 Dec. 1883.

[58] CO 267/358, Minute by Hemming on Rowe to CO, 24 June 1885. CO 267/361, Minute by Hemming on Manchester CC to CO, 21 May 1885. CO 96/154, Minute by Hemming on Manchester CC to CO, 7 Dec. 1883.

[59] See below.

[60] *PMCC*, 18 Feb. 1884; 4 April 1884. FO 84/1684, Manchester CC to FO, 4 April 1884.

[61] *PMCC*, 16 Sept. 1885. FO 84/1742, Manchester CC to FO, 16 Sept. 1885. CO 96/169, same to same, 16 Sept. 1885.

[62] *LWAS*, 9 Sept. 1885. FO 84/1742, London CC to FO, 17 Sept. 1885. CO 96/169, London CC to CO, 17 Sept. 1885.

[63] CO 96/169, Goldie to Sir Julian Pauncefote, 18 June 1885 enclosed in National African Company to CO, 25 Sept. 1885.

[64] *PMCC*, 26 Nov. 1884. *LWAS*, 2 Dec. 1884. CO 96/154, Manchester CC to CO, 7 Dec. 1883.

[65] R. Oliver, *Sir Harry Johnston and the Scramble for Africa*, London, 1957, pp. 66–72. FO 84/1680, Holmwood to Granville, 20 Nov. 1884. *Proceedings of the Royal Geographical Society*, vi (1884), pp. 670–710, cited in M. E. Chamberlain, 'Clement Hill's Memoranda and the British Interest in East Africa', *English Historical Review*, lxxxvii, July 1972, p. 537.

[66] M. J. de Kiewiet, 'History of the Imperial British East Africa Company, 1876–95', Ph.D. thesis, London, 1955, pp. 61–2.

[67] J. S. Galbraith, *Mackinnon and East Africa 1878–95*, pp. 87–8.

A. Ramm (ed.), *The Political Correspondence of Mr. Gladstone and Lord Granville 1876–86*, Oxford, 1962, II, pp. 294–5. Chamberlain, *English Historical Review*, lxxxvii, July 1972, p. 539.

[68] *PMCC*, 28 Jan. 1885; 25 March 1885. *MG*, 3 Feb. 1885.

[69] FO 84/1737, Holmwood to Hutton, 10 April 1885, enclosed in Hutton to Granville, 20 April 1885.

[70] *PMCC*, 20 April 1885. FO 84/1737, Hutton to Granville, 20 April 1885.

[71] FO 84/1737, Aberdare *et al.* to Granville, 22 April 1885.

[72] FO 84/1737, Aberdare to Granville, 24 April 1885. FO 84/1738, John Slagg to Granville, 12 May 1885. *MP*, Hutton to Mackinnon, 3 July 1885; same to same, 11 July 1885; same to same, 24 July 1885.

[73] *PMCC*, 15 July 1885. FO 84/1740, Manchester CC to FO, 15 July 1885.

[74] *PMCC*, 15 July 1885. FO 84/1740, John Slagg to FO, 16 July 1885. *MP*, Hutton to Mackinnon, 24 July 1885.

[75] *MG*, 5 Aug. 1885.

[76] FO 84/1711, Granville to Malet, 25 May 1885.

[77] See Chamberlain, *English Historical Review*, lxxxvii, July 1972, p. 543.

[78] See De Kiewiet, 'History of the Imperial East Africa Company', p. 70. Galbraith, *Mackinnon and East Africa*, p. 100.

[79] *MP*, Johnston to Hutton, 31 Oct. 1885.

[80] *PMCC*, 4 Nov. 1885.

Six

International competition and imperial expansion in the late 1880s

The British economy entered another expansionary phase around 1886. Exports rose by 22 per cent between 1886 and 1890, while gross domestic product increased by 20 per cent between 1885 and 1890.[1] However, many British businessmen recovered only gradually from the pessimism of the mid 1880s. It was not until the last two years of the decade that there was anything like a buoyant mood in business circles. Even then confidence was tempered with considerable caution. The slump of 1883–6 had followed hard on the heels of the economic difficulties of the late 1870s and the gradualness of the post-1886 recovery left many businessmen hesitant and doubtful. Indeed there were some who believed that British trade and industry would never again be quite so comfortable as they had been in the prosperous decades of the mid nineteenth century. If British commercial supremacy was not yet a thing of the past, it was for many businessmen something that could no longer be taken for granted in the future.

In addition to its gradualness, the post-1886 recovery was marred by certain other disquieting features. For the chief textile trades in particular, prospects were not encouraging; exports of wool textiles scarcely rose at all, mainly because of a decrease in European and American demand, and despite improvements in the short run, the long-term outlook for the cotton industry was bleak in the late 1880s. Industrialisation in Europe and the United States cut demand from these regions at the same time as Manchester became alarmed over growing competition in the Far East, particularly from India.[2] On the other hand, the shipping trades generally fared well in the late eighties, although Liverpool steamship interests suffered from a mild slump in 1885–7.[3]

All Britain's export trades faced increasing challenges from foreign competition in the late eighties. Many suffered also from the effects of a fresh round of tariff increases in Europe in the second half of the decade. The new Italian tariff of 1887, for example, was particularly effective in excluding foreign competition from the Italian market; it virtually wiped out the export of British cottons and brought about a sharp decline in the exports of British woollens to Italy.[4] Although British merchants and manufacturers protested strongly against the new tariff, they were pessimistic about their chances of persuading the Italian Government to change its mind.[5] The American McKinley tariff, introduced in 1890, further dampened the hopes of British free-traders. Moreover, as the tempo of French expansion in Africa and Asia increased in the late 1880s, British merchants became increasingly concerned that they would be shut out of any territories that France might take under her protection. Finding it more and more difficult to penetrate traditional European and American markets, British merchants began to fear that they would soon be shut out of the neutral markets of the world as well.

Though British businessmen became increasingly aware of their kinsmen in Canada, Australia and New Zealand in the second half of the 1880s, it seems doubtful that this new consciousness of the empire of settlement was directly related to business conditions in the metropolis. Rather, it seems more to have been a part of the general quickening of interest in the self-governing colonies among British politicians, journalists and prominent public figures in the late 1880s.[6] It is unlikely that there was ever any large section of the British public in favour of the separation of the settlement colonies, at least since 1870,[7] but it was not until the mid 1880s that there emerged substantial public interest in strengthening and consolidating the ties between England and the self-governing colonies. The movement for imperial unity that developed in the 1880s was shaped chiefly by nationalistic and racialist sentiments about the history and future prospects of Anglo-Saxons overseas. Such feelings found eloquent expression in John Seeley's Cambridge lectures on *The Expansion of England* and James A. Froude's *Oceana*, both published in the mid 1880s. Imperial sentiments were also stirred by the agitation over Irish Home Rule and the foundation of the Imperial Federation League in 1884.

Since its foundation in the early 1880s, the London Chamber of

Commerce took a keen interest in the settlement colonies. In 1885 the Chamber invited representatives of chambers of commerce throughout the Empire to a congress timed to coincide with the Colonial and Indian Exhibition in the summer of 1886. Response to the London invitation in the self-governing colonies was highly encouraging and in July 1886 delegates from ninety-seven British, colonial and Indian chambers of commerce assembled in the conference room of the Colonial and Indian Exhibition in South Kensington. There was a high degree of agreement among the delegates when the conference tackled certain technical questions of trade like the codification of commercial law throughout the Empire and the establishment of a uniform postal rate. However, little was said about the issue of imperial unity except that most businessmen were vaguely in favour of it.[8]

As the congress proceeded it became apparent that while the chief impetus in the commercial world for imperial unity came from the colonial side, British business opinion was very much in favour of a general strengthening of the bonds between Britain and the settlement colonies. Despite their complaints against colonial tariffs, British merchants did not regard these as insuperable obstacles to imperial unity. This was chiefly because they thought of the Empire and its consolidation in terms of politics or defence; commercial union was not regarded by British businessmen as a pre-requisite for, or even something necessarily connected with, the unity of the Empire.

Some mercantile advocates of closer commercial relations within the Empire laid particular emphasis on the value of the colonial trade to the British economy. It was argued that the per capita consumption of British goods in the colonies of settlement was much higher than in the United States or Europe. Moreover, the colonial trade tended generally to expand during bouts of recession and therefore exerted a stabilising influence on the British economy.[9] Such arguments attracted some attention after 1890 with the onset of another slump in business activity but they did not achieve wide currency in the late 1880s. Merchants in Glasgow, Liverpool, London and Manchester looked to the whole world as their market and supplier of raw materials. Only in Birmingham and some of the smaller industrial towns was there strong support for an imperial customs union as the basis for a federation of the British Empire. The idea of granting preferential tariff treatment to the colonies, implying as it did a revolution in British commercial policy, could command little support among the majority of British merchants. Free trade remained for most British merchants the ark of the covenant of economic orthodoxy. The Annual Meeting of the Association of U.K. Chambers of Commerce in 1888 rejected by an 'overwhelming majority' a resolution in favour of preferential tariffs for the colonies.[10] While most businessmen were in favour of strengthening the ties of empire, it was not to commerce that they looked for the unifying and solidifying agent; imperial unity was regarded more as a matter of politics or national security than an economic issue.

Mercantile interest in India, on the other hand, was much more a matter of economic self-interest. A levelling off in the long-term rate of expansion of Indian demand for British textiles was one of the chief factors that darkened the outlook of the cotton industry in the second half of the 1880s. The cotton duties had been blamed for the slump in Indian consumption of British textiles in the late seventies, but since these had been repealed in 1882, they could not be held to blame for the stagnancy of Indian demand in the second half of the 1880s. Perhaps other more fundamental factors were at work. A special committee of the Manchester Chamber of Commerce was appointed in 1887 to inquire 'as to the causes and circumstances which have . . . enabled Bombay spinners to supersede those of Lancashire'.[11] Although the committee failed to agree on the reasons why Manchester was losing ground in the Indian market, its inquiry revealed incidentally that the working week in the Indian mills was seventy-four hours or more. This led some Manchester businessmen to argue that in the interests of fair competition and, they hastened to add, the welfare of the Indian labourer, the English factory laws relating to hours of labour of women and children ought to be enforced in India. Britain, they said, should use imperial authority to secure the enforcement of factory legislation in India. There was some pressure upon the government from Lancashire in 1888 for factory labour legislation in India, though it fell short of a concerted commercial campaign such as the cotton interests had mounted over the Indian cotton duties.[12] At the same time, however, their uneasiness over the static position of British exports to India made Lancashire merchants and manufacturers highly receptive to proposals for opening new markets elsewhere as a kind of insurance against the day when the

Indian market finally slipped away. As in the late 1870s, uncertainty over the Indian market was an important factor in stimulating Lancashire's interest in securing new overseas outlets in Africa. There was no further commercial pressure for intervention in China in the late 1880s. After reaching a peak in 1885, mercantile agitation for a trade route from Burma to south-western China subsided. The advocates of a back door into the allegedly rich Chinese market continued to canvass British commercial circles for support but mercantile interest in the idea failed to reach the level of the late 1870s or the mid 1880s. The leading British chambers of commerce continued to advocate the opening of trade connections between Burma and south-western China but neither the number nor the enthusiasm of their representations to government reached the levels of earlier times.[13] This was of course partly because of the annexation of Upper Burma in 1886 and the government's subsequent decision to survey a railway route from Mandalay to the Chinese frontier. The business world's lack of interest in a Burma route to China in the late 1880s also reflected improved economic conditions in Britain. Perhaps even more important was the fact that despite growing European rivalry in China, now the focus of European interest in the Far East, that contest had not yet turned into a scramble for pieces of the Celestial Kingdom itself.

The importance of international competition for existing and potential markets as a primary motive of European expansionism in the late 1880s is apparent when we turn to Africa. Here the contrast with the Far East is striking. While continuing economic uncertainty in Britain led businessmen to press for government intervention in Africa in the late 1880s, the upswing in the trade cycle did much to lessen this commercial pressure. The main driving force behind commercial imperialism was a fear of being shut out of potentially valuable markets by hostile foreign tariffs. The areas of concern to British businessmen in these years were almost exclusively those where foreign rivalry threatened to destroy existing trade or cut off potentially rich markets, such as West Africa. East Africa, on the other hand, where there was no such threat, attracted scarcely any attention in British business circles.

In addition to the threat of protectionist foreign powers—chiefly France—in West Africa, there were several other factors which accounted for commercial interest in that region in the late 1880s. The exclusive trading practices of the Royal Niger Company were beginning to stir up considerable opposition among businessmen in Britain. At first this was confined largely to those merchants directly affected by the Niger Company's monopolistic practices, most of whom belonged to the African Trade Section of the Liverpool Chamber of Commerce. Although commercial circles in Britain refrained from a general onslaught on the Niger Company, proposals to place the Oil Rivers under chartered company rule were vigorously opposed by most of the leading chambers of commerce on free-trade grounds. Once again doctrinaire free-trade arguments were used to support demands for direct imperial intervention.

Another factor that attracted commercial attention to West Africa in the late 1880s was the increased agitation of local British merchants for government intervention in the West African interior. While the circumstances of trade varied along different parts of the coast, merchants throughout West Africa faced a common set of problems in the second half of the 1880s. Throughout the whole of the nineteenth century world prices for the two most important West African staples, palm oil and palm kernels, underwent a protracted decline. While this reflected a world-wide trend in raw material prices generally and a reduction in ocean freight rates, it was also the result of an increase in the total world supply of mineral and vegetable oils. The exploitation of petroleum resources in the United States in the 1860s and, following the opening of the Suez Canal in 1869, the entry into the market of Indian groundnuts and Australian tallow tended to depress world prices for fats and oils.[14] This tendency was increased by a general slackening of world demand for mineral and vegetable oils caused chiefly by recessions and economic uncertainty in the industrialised countries in the closing decades of the nineteenth century. From an average of £37 per ton in 1861–5 the European price for palm oil fell to £20 per ton in 1886–90. In the same period prices for palm kernels fell from an average of £15 a ton to just over £10 a ton.[15] While the advent of the steamship to the West African shipping trade reduced freight rates to England, this only partly offset the effect of falling prices. Moreover, the steamship tended to increase competition in the West African trade. African merchants no longer had to possess their own ships or join with others to charter vessels; those with limited capital could now ship small amounts of cargo on a regular basis using the independent lines.

Because they were unable to reduce their costs as fast as prices fell, most West African merchants found themselves in a severe profit squeeze by the late 1880s. Many firms resorted to drastic expedients to improve their financial position. European merchants attempted to fix produce prices paid to African middlemen by combination among themselves. They also sought to obtain higher prices for the commodities they imported into West Africa, sometimes resorting to adulteration of their goods in a desperate effort to increase their profit margins. Some firms attempted to increase their turnover, hoping to reduce losses by increased sales. Almost invariably these practices brought them into conflict with African producers, who fiercely resisted attempts to pass on lower prices. The Africans frequently retaliated by adulterating produce or withholding supplies in attempts to jack up the price. These practices became increasingly frequent and bitter during the late 1880s and early 1890s.[16]

It has often been noted that most European merchants in West Africa were prepared to accept the African middleman system.[17] This was essentially a trading practice in which Europeans for the most part stayed on the coasts and conducted their trade through African merchants who in turn dealt with other Africans farther in the interior. Few European merchants were prepared to extend their operations into the interior because of the high risks involved. While this is generally correct, it tends to play down the fact that many African merchants were anxious for the commercial penetration of the West African hinterland if only the government would undertake to provide the 'necessary' support. By the late 1880s their desire for increased commercial penetration of the African interior was tending to overshadow the merchants' natural repugnance to increased taxation and regulation. What African merchants wanted in the late 1880s was usually summed up in their frequent demands for 'law and order' in the interior. By this they really meant the use of British political and military power to put an end to warfare among rival African polities that was impeding the free flow of trade, to secure the abolition of internal African tolls and taxes on trade and guarantee the enforcement of commercial contracts and the payment of debts. Though few recognised it at the time, these demands amounted to nothing less than a direct challenge to the territorial integrity and political independence of many of the African kingdoms and states in the region.

94

With economic uncertainty in Britain, increased anxiety over foreign competition and foreign tariffs and the danger that European powers would carve out exclusive trading areas in Africa, commercial opinion in the metropolis was highly supportive of the interventionist arguments of the African merchants. This conjunction of factors underlay commercial interest in West Africa in the 1880s. Above all it was the fear of losing potentially valuable markets to foreign rivals that led businessmen in Britain to support the African merchants in their clamour for government intervention in the interior. Where this factor was not relevant, as in East Africa, or where it remained relatively weak, as in South Africa, businessmen in the metropolis were little concerned with events in the 'Dark Continent'. Moreover, it was in those particular areas of West Africa where commercial opinion in the metropolis supported the demands of local African merchants for state intervention, the Gold Coast and Lagos, that the British Government ultimately intervened. Conversely, it was largely the lack of support in business circles in the metropolis at the crucial moment of delimitation negotiations that permitted the government to ignore the clamour of British merchants in the Gambia and Sierra Leone for the preservation of their hinterlands in the late 1880s.

Like their counterparts elsewhere in West Africa, British merchants in the Colonies of Sierra Leone and the Gambia pressed for the establishment of 'law and order' in districts beyond British jurisdiction where, they alleged, internecine warfare among Africans was disrupting the normal course of trade. In October 1888 Sir John Hay, the new Governor of Sierra Leone, was present at a special meeting of the Manchester Chamber of Commerce attended by about thirty African merchants from Manchester and Liverpool. What British merchants required in Africa, according to Mr Sykes of the firm of Sykes, Callander and Co., was 'that the Government will give to their representatives there such power that they will be able to quell disturbances upon their breaking out'.[18] Other merchants suggested to Hay that the government take possession of some prominent points on the coasts or rivers and declare them to be British territory. As Mr Edwards of Messrs Edwards Bros. put it, 'we want a few soldiers there to make the people a little afraid of us'.[19] The interview made a considerable impression on the new Governor. He assured the merchants that 'the interests of the Government and the interests of the merchants are identical, i.e., the prosperity and welfare of the Colony . . . without peace we shall have no trade. . . .'.[20]

In the same month the Liverpool Chamber of Commerce supported an urgent request for protection from certain African kings and chiefs in the neighbourhood of Sierra Leone.

These mercantile concerns were not reflected in the official Anglo-French negotiations which began early in the following year. The Foreign Office concluded a comprehensive boundary agreement with France, the Anglo-French Convention of 10 August 1889, which in effect prevented both the Gambia and Sierra Leone from becoming any more than coastal enclaves.[21] However, British merchants did not press the issue again at that time. When they learned of the Convention later in the year, the Liverpool and Manchester Chambers of Commerce merely inquired at the Colonial Office for information on its details. They had no inkling of the scope of its provisions. Until the 1890s there was no serious mercantile pressure for territorial expansion in the region of Sierra Leone. Unlike the situation in the Gold Coast and the region of Lagos, where powerful metropolitan commercial groups pressed for government intervention in the interior, there was no strong or sustained mercantile pressure to extend British influence inland in the region of the Gambia or Sierra Leone in the second half of the 1880s. There was of course pressure from British merchants in the colonies themselves, but without firm backing from metropolitan businessmen this was insufficient to move the government. Some of the leading chambers of commerce took up the cry of the Sierra Leone merchants in the early 1890s when the extent of France's gains in the region became public knowledge but by then it was too late.

In the second half of the 1880s British merchants in the Gold Coast also began to clamour for government intervention in the interior, particularly in the Kingdom of Ashanti. They complained that disturbed political conditions in Ashanti were disrupting British trade routes to the interior.[22] When the Colonial Office appeared reluctant to take any decisive action against Ashanti, the Gold Coast merchants attempted to force the government to move by mobilising commercial opinion in Britain. At the instigation of the Gold Coast merchants, the West African Section of the London Chamber of Commerce set up a committee to inquire into the state of affairs in Ashanti. Upon its recommendations the Chamber subsequently urged the Colonial Office to appoint a British Resident at Kumasi, the Ashanti capital, to ensure the peaceful settlement of disputes and the uninterrupted flow of trade with the coast. Getting no satisfaction from the government, the London merchants pressed the Colonial Office again later in the year.[23]

It was not only conditions in Ashanti that led to mercantile agitation over the Gold Coast. In 1887 the London Chamber of Commerce complained of the Sefwi chiefs who

> from their position on the border of the Colony were able to stop all communication between the coast and the tribes lying beyond themselves. By these means they were able to take the place formerly occupied by the Ashantees and to act as middlemen between the European trade and the interior.[24]

Similar complaints were made by the Liverpool and Manchester Chambers of Commerce around the same time.[25] Increasingly impatient of the middleman system, British merchants were demanding that the government intervene to open up free trade markets in the interior.

The despatch of a travelling commissioner to Ashanti and the government's promise that the inclusion of Sefwi within the Protectorate would receive 'serious consideration' reassured the merchants for a time.[26] It was not long, however, before the government's inactivity raised serious doubts in the minds of the British merchants whether officials were in fact doing all they could to promote the development of trade in the Gold Coast. Towards the end of 1887, the Manchester Chamber of Commerce transmitted to the Colonial Office further complaints from Gold Coast merchants about disturbed conditions in the interior. Around the same time the London Chamber reiterated its earlier demands for the appointment of a British Resident at the Ashanti capital.[27] Though the Colonial Office still refused to take this step because of fears of the risks and expenditure it would entail, the government was by this time coming round to the view that something would have to be done to satisfy commercial demands for the extension of British influence in the Gold Coast.

It was the threat of French pre-emption of what British merchants regarded as their 'natural' hinterlands in the region of Lagos that prompted the government to move in the late 1880s. At first the Foreign Office hoped to maintain a standstill arrangement with

France in the region, pending a general Anglo-French treaty on West Africa. However, British merchants at Lagos began to clamour for direct intervention in Yorubaland. The merchants complained that incessant warfare among the Yoruba was disrupting the trade of Lagos. They also feared that the French would use their nearby base of Porto Novo to draw off Yoruba produce or, worse still, to extend their own political influence into Yorubaland.[28]

These fears appeared to be confirmed in 1888 when a French expedition, headed by Captain Viard, concluded a treaty of trade and friendship with Abeokuta, an important commercial centre behind Lagos. Since Abeokuta had long been a focus of British missionary and commercial attention, the Lagos mercantile community—African as well as European—urged the British Government to take decisive action to counteract the French activity, particularly by concluding treaties with the more important African states in the Lagos hinterland.[29] The government still hoped to maintain British influence in Yorubaland without any further treaty-making; instead, the Colonial Office asked the Foreign Secretary to appeal to the French Government not to ratify the Viard treaty, on the grounds that it violated the Anglo-French informal standstill agreement. At the same time the Governor of Lagos was instructed not to accept the offer of cession of their lands already made by chiefs in certain of the interior districts.[30] Not wishing themselves to become involved in Yorubaland, the British Government still hoped to keep the French out on the basis of their earlier gentlemen's agreement.

Such a solution was no longer satisfactory to mercantile opinion in the Colony and in Britain. The Lagos merchants at first attempted to put pressure on the colonial government but when it became apparent that the Governor could not act without authority from London, they shifted their campaign to the home front. To strengthen their case for intervention they sought to mobilise commercial opinion in Britain.

In July, at the request of the Lagos merchants, the Liverpool Chamber of Commerce asked the Colonial Office what steps it planned to take to protect British trade in Yorubaland. The government's reply that the Foreign Office was in communication with France and the Governor on the subject failed to satisfy the Liverpool businessmen.[31] By 1888 Liverpool's interest in West African commerce extended far beyond the circle of those directly involved in the trade itself. A special meeting of the African Trade Section of the Liverpool Chamber of Commerce on 11 July to consider the Abeokuta question attracted widespread attention in the Liverpool mercantile community. George Hutchinson, Chairman of the African Trade Section, informed the meeting that French possession of Abeokuta would be ruinous to the trade of Lagos, since the French would divert a major part of the trade of the interior to their own coastal possessions. The Liverpool Chamber appointed a deputation, representing the entire Chamber and headed by the President H. Coke, to interview the Colonial Secretary. At the same time the Liverpool merchants wrote to the Chambers of Commerce of Glasgow, London and Manchester asking for their support.[32]

By now aware of the strength of mercantile feeling on the subject of Abeokuta, the Colonial Office requested the Foreign Office 'to protest most strongly' to the French against the Viard treaty.[33] Meanwhile, commercial pressure steadily mounted. The Manchester merchants promised to join Liverpool's deputation to the Colonial Office fixed for 25 July; at the same time they requested the attendance of the three Manchester M.P.s.[34] The Glasgow merchants also promised their support. In a letter to the Colonial Office on 23 July, the President of the Glasgow Chamber of Commerce reminded the government that 'Lagos is one of the most important Colonies on the west Coast of Africa, and is a large market for British manufactures'.[35] The French action at Abeokuta, he said, would directly threaten the prosperity of that Colony. The following day the Liverpool Chamber informed the Colonial Office that the attempts of foreign powers to exclude British trade from their territories made it necessary for Britain

> generally to encourage kings and chiefs of districts adjoining British possessions to make treaties with Her Majesty's Government whereby British trade and the influence accompanying it would be fostered and secured in such a manner that iniquitous competition on the part of other Powers would cease to exist.[36]

On 26 July an impressive deputation of Liverpool and Manchester merchants and M.P.s met Knutsford at the Colonial Office. H. Coke, President of the Liverpool Chamber, pointed out to the Colonial Secretary that while British merchants were prepared to meet foreign competition anywhere on an equal footing, they found it necessary to seek government support against the 'unfair' trade policy of the French. Other members of the deputation stressed the fact that the West African trade involved very substantial shipping and commercial interests in Britain. Manchester merchants pointed out how important it was for the cotton trade that 'all the markets they had at present should be kept open'.[37]

This mercantile pressure soon bore fruit. After considerable prompting from the Colonial Office, the Foreign Office elicited a statement from the French to the effect that while the French Government acknowledged Viard as its agent, his mission was of a purely commercial nature and that they would not ratify any of the political clauses of the Abeokuta treaty.[38] Not wishing to take any chances, the Colonial Office now allowed Governor Moloney to conclude a number of treaties with African authorities in the Lagos hinterland. Although these were not explicitly acknowledged by the British Government, they could serve as bargaining counters in any subsequent negotiations with the French. The Colonial Office also pressed the Foreign Office to open discussions with the French for a general settlement of their respective claims in West Africa.[39]

The negotiations were slow to start, since the Foreign Office preferred to wait for the French to make the opening proposals for a settlement. Meanwhile, merchants in London and Manchester pressed for a general Anglo-French agreement defining spheres of influence in West Africa. The West African Section of the London Chamber of Commerce revived that Chamber's 1885 proposals for the 'consolidation of the colonial possessions of various European powers in Western Africa'.[40] Through informal interviews with officials of the Foreign and Colonial Offices, the London Chamber urged the government to partition spheres of influence with the French in West Africa. At the same time, the London merchants began to mobilise commercial opinion throughout the country.[41]

The negotiations with France finally got under way early in 1889 and culminated in the Anglo-French Convention in August of that year. Although there was a brief flurry of commercial agitation in June 1889, after rumours circulated of French plans to annex Abeokuta, the fate of that town was never really in doubt. While the 1889 agreement with France did not meet the wishes of the African merchants at all points, it did satisfy commercial opinion in Britain. To be sure, businessmen were unaware of the gains made by France in the region of Sierra Leone;[42] by greatly restricting the limits within which the Gambia and Sierra Leone could expand, the 1889 agreement virtually ensured that these two colonies could never be any more than coastal enclaves with limited economic potential. The 1889 agreement defined the western boundary of the Gold Coast for only twenty miles inland. Farther south it defined the boundary between Lagos and Porto Novo. In neither case did the agreement preclude the possibility of French or British penetration of the regions behind the other's coastal spheres. It did, however, provide a respite in local Anglo-French rivalry in West Africa and it satisfied the demands of metropolitan business interests for the creation of British spheres of influence in the coastal regions of the Gold Coast and Lagos.

South of the West African colonies, in the region of the Niger River, the British Government had revived an eighteenth-century colonial device and granted a Royal Charter to the Niger Company in 1886. By the terms of the Charter the company acquired sweeping powers over the vast basin of the Niger River. It was largely because the British Government wished to avoid involving itself in the Niger region that it granted such wide powers to the company, which it was hoped would act as a protective umbrella for British interests in the region. It was not long, however, before the company drew heavy criticism from African merchants in Liverpool. It was charged—with considerable justification—that the company was using the Charter to create a trade monopoly in the Niger basin. For a time it appeared as if there would be a major commercial campaign against the Royal Niger Company, similar perhaps to that against the Anglo-Portuguese Congo Treaty a few years earlier; but in the case of the Niger the commercial opposition failed to materialise. The Liverpool African Association, which led the clamour against the Niger Company in the beginning, soon changed its mind about mounting a challenge to the company's Charter. By the beginning of 1888 the African Association was deeply involved in negotiations with the Niger Company for a fusion of their interests on the Niger and the extension of the company's Charter to the Oil Rivers. Because of this, the Liverpool Chamber's protests against the Niger Company in April 1888 were restricted to complaints against particular administrative acts of the Company; there were no demands for a revocation of the Charter.[43]

However, the Liverpool Chamber of Commerce soon began to challenge the whole conception of chartered company rule in West Africa. By the second half of the 1880s, the smaller merchants outside the African Association and the growing number of commission houses made up the bulk of the membership of the African Trade Section of the Liverpool Chamber of Commerce, now one of the most powerful commercial lobbies in Lancashire. The interests of the African steamship companies coincided generally with those of the smaller African firms and the commission houses; the steamship owners feared that if ever the Niger Company managed to secure a complete monopoly of the Niger trade, it would be only a matter of time before they would establish their own shipping line.[44] Moreover, any attempt to obtain exclusive commercial advantages in Africa would be almost certain to be opposed by most Liverpool businessmen on doctrinaire free-trade grounds.

When the negotiations between the Royal Niger Company and the African Association broke down, towards the end of 1888, the latter made plans to obtain a separate charter for the Oil Rivers. By this time, however, African merchants outside the Association, together with the steamship owners, had organised strong opposition within the African Trade Section of the Liverpool Chamber of Commerce. The shipping companies could also count on the support of the powerful shipping lobby in the House of Commons.[45]

By the late 1880s the Liverpool Chamber of Commerce was pressing for greater government involvement in the hinterlands of the Gold Coast and Lagos. When free trade in these regions seemed to be endangered by foreign powers the merchants did not hesitate to call upon the British Government for intervention. It was hardly surprising therefore that in view of the accusations of monopoly levelled against the Niger Company, Liverpool merchants would not wish to see a large section of the African coastline under chartered company rule. If it was important that the African hinterlands remain open to all traders, it was even more essential that there be no impediments to the free movement of imports and exports in the coastal regions through which the trade of the interior must pass. Rejecting the Niger Company's claim that the huge expenditures and high risks involved in opening up the Niger region required the resources of a chartered company, the Liverpool merchants informed the Colonial Office that the granting of a charter for the Oil Rivers would be 'a breach of the trade principles of this nation'.[46] Instead, they urged the government to establish a Crown Colony or at least a British protectorate administration in the Oil Rivers district. This opposition to an Oil Rivers charter in early 1890 showed clearly that mercantile opinion was no longer willing to accept the chartered company as an instrument for opening new markets in Africa. The restrictive trading practices of chartered company rule no less than the protectionist policies of some of the continental powers were leading British businessmen to the conclusion that the preservation of free trade in Africa might require the establishment of formal protectorates or even crown colonies.

For businessmen in Britain the east coast of Africa stood in striking contrast to West Africa. One of the main reasons why British businessmen pressed for government intervention in West Africa after 1886 was their fear that France was seeking to extend her protectionist trading system in that part of the world. There was no such anxiety over East Africa after about 1886, since Britain's chief rival in that region, Germany, adhered to free trade. Despite considerable local Anglo-French rivalry in East Africa in the late 1880s, mercantile opinion in Britain remained largely unconcerned. The directors of the Glasgow Chamber of Commerce, for example, appear totally to have ignored German colonial activity in East Africa. On the other hand, a treaty forced upon Madagascar by the French in 1886 led to anxious inquiries at the Foreign Office as to whether the French action might interfere with British trading and treaty rights on that island. It was likewise in 1890 when Britain and Germany completed the process of partitioning East Africa.[47] By contrast with the Anglo-French discussions over West Africa in the late 1880s, the Anglo-German negotiations leading to the East Africa agreement of 1890—the so-called Heligoland Treaty—received scant notice in British commercial circles.

Despite the rapid economic changes in southern Africa following the discovery of the Witwatersrand gold reef in 1886 and the relatively large share of South Africa in Britain's trade with the African continent, mercantile interest in South Africa remained relatively weak. Unlike the situation in West Africa, where trade was the predominant economic motive at work, southern Africa attracted fairly large amounts of direct British investment. Financial interests, establishing themselves chiefly in the Cape Colony, sometimes clashed with commercial and missionary interests centred in the metropolis.[48]

This dichotomy emerged most sharply in Bechuanaland in 1884–5. Ever since the 1860s British missionaries working among the Tswana hoped to persuade the British Government to discharge 'the public obligations of humanity and justice' by protecting 'the peaceful and prosperous civilisation which the labour of two generations of Christian missionaries had produced in Bechuanaland'.[49] Their campaign gathered momentum in the 1880s, particularly after the foundation in 1883 of the South African Committee, a small though influential group of humanitarians, missionaries and businessmen headed by John Mackenzie and Joseph Chamberlain. The missionaries and their allies in Britain faced stiff opposition from financial and agricultural interests in the Cape Colony. Led by Cecil Rhodes, Cape colonial interests sought to persuade the Cape Ministry to annex Bechuanaland, thereby pre-empting the 'imperial factor' and ensuring that expansion northwards proceeded under colonial auspices. The first round in this contest went to the missionaries and their supporters in the metropolis when the British Government declared a Protectorate in Bechuanaland in 1885.[50]

Flushed by this success, the missionary Mackenzie and the South African Committee embarked on a campaign to gather support in Britain for further imperial intervention in South Africa. Their main demand was for imperial as opposed to colonial administration in the parts of southern Africa already occupied by white settlers and the extension of British rule to the Zambezi River. Appealing to commercial opinion in Britain, Mackenzie advocated a policy of direct imperial responsibility and development in the Transkei, Pondoland, Basutoland, Swaziland, Amatongaland and Bechuanaland. The most notable success of the British imperialists came in 1888 when the Chambers of Commerce of Edinburgh, Glasgow and London called upon the British Government to extend its influence in the 'trans-colonial territories' in southern Africa.[51] Mackenzie's supporters had good reason for satisfaction in July 1888 when the British Government officially declared that it considered the whole of southern Zambesia to be 'exclusively within the British sphere of influence'.[52]

There was a growing feeling in business circles that within this sphere of influence greater government activity was required.

As William Dunn, a prominent London merchant, said in April 1889:

> It has now become necessary for the Colonial Office to show more activity than was indicated with the mere definition of spheres of influence. What this country wanted was not spheres of influence but an active protectorate. Government ... had too long gone on with a waiting policy.[53]

For a time it appeared that commercial opinion in Britain might mount a campaign to force the British Government to intervene in Swaziland, which in 1889 came under considerable pressure from the Transvaal Boers who looked upon that African territory as an outlet on the Indian Ocean. During 1889 several leading British chambers of commerce urged the government to take steps to keep Swaziland out of the hands of the Boers.[54]

This metropolitan-based commercial imperialism remained relatively weak, however, and it received a powerful check by economic forces emanating from southern Africa itself. There is no need here to detail the complex political manœuvrings by which Cecil Rhodes got a charter for his British South Africa Company. The important point is that the government's decision in favour of the charter in May 1889 meant that British policy was to a large extent committed to supporting Rhodes. This fact goes far to explain why in Swaziland the British Government adopted the policy advocated by the South African High Commissioner, Sir Hercules Robinson. Robinson was completely under the influence of Rhodes and Jan Hofmeyr, the leader of the Cape Dutch party, who were in favour of letting the Transvaal Boers take Swaziland in return for a promise to keep out of Matabeleland, in which Rhodes was interested, and to join the Cape customs union.[55] South African financial and agricultural interests were in this case able to block commercial pressure in Britain. Economic imperialism in South Africa emanated not from the metropolis but chiefly from settler mining and agricultural interests. The metropolitan-based commercial imperialism that operated in parts of West and East Africa made some headway in southern Africa but it found itself blocked by an even more powerful economic imperialism emanating from the white settler community within the colony itself.

Notes

[1] Calculated from Feinstein, *National Income, Expenditure and Output of the United Kingdom 1855–1965*, Table 3, col. 2 and Table 4, col. 5.

[2] Saul, *British Overseas Trade*, pp. 105–6.

[3] Hyde, *Liverpool and the Mersey*, p. 97.

[4] Saul, *British Overseas Trade*, pp. 149, 156.

[5] See, for example, *RBCC*, 1887. *MG*, 1 Nov. 1887.

[6] R. Koebner, *Imperialism: The Story and Significance of a Political Word*, Cambridge, 1964, pp. 166–93.

[7] This topic remains highly controversial. For a good analysis of the considerable amount of recent literature on the subject, see ch. I of C. C. Eldridge, *England's Mission: The Imperial Idea in the Age of Gladstone and Disraeli, 1868–1880*, London, 1973.

[8] See *Proceedings of the First Congress of the Chambers of Commerce of the Empire*, London, 1886.

[9] See, for example, G. Baden-Powell, 'The Commercial Relations of the British Empire', *CCJ*, Supp., 6 June 1887.

[10] *RACC*, Feb. 1888.

[11] *PMCC*, 31 Oct. 1887.

[12] See *PMCC*, 21 May 1890; 22 Sept. 1890; 18 Oct. 1890. *RACC*, Sept. 1888.

[13] See *MBCC*, 30 March 1887; 26 May 1887. *MLCC*, 23 March 1887. *MGCC*, 14 Nov. 1887. *CCJ*, 5 Nov. 1887, Supp.

[14] Allan McPhee, *The Economic Revolution in British West Africa*, London, 1926.

[15] A. G. Hopkins, *An Economic History of West Africa*, London, 1973, p. 133.

[16] *Ibid.*, ch. 4, and the same author's 'Economic Imperialism in West Africa: Lagos 1880–92', *EcHR*, 2nd ser., xxi, 1968, pp. 580–606.

[17] See, for example, Obaro Ikime, *Merchant Prince of the Niger Delta*, London, 1968, pp. 73–5.

[18] *PMCC*, 4 Oct. 1888. CO 267/373, Manchester CC to CO, 2 Nov. 1888.

[19] *Ibid.*

[20] *Ibid.*

[21] E. Hertslet, *Map of Africa by Treaty*, London, 1896, M. 11, No. 110. Although Sierre Leone expanded in the 1890s, the 1889 Anglo-French Convention imposed definite limits to this.

²² See, for example, CO 879/321, F. D. Swanzy to CO, 8 April 1886. CO/178, J. Hutton to CO, 9 Nov. 1886. See also David Kimble, *A Political History of Ghana*, Oxford, 1963, pp. 274–80.
²³ *LWAS*, 8 April 1886; 21 April 1886; 18 Nov. 1886. CO 96/178, London CC to CO, 22 April 1886; same to same, 24 Nov. 1886.
²⁴ *LWAS*, 12 Jan. 1887.
²⁵ CO 879/25/333, Liverpool CC to CO, 11 March 1887; Manchester CC to CO, 8 Feb. 1887; same to same, 28 Feb. 1887.
²⁶ *LDC*, 31 March 1887. *LWAS*, 4 Oct. 1887.
²⁷ *PMCC*, 11 Oct. 1887. CO 96/187, Manchester CC to CO and encl., 12 Oct. 1887. *LWAS*, 20 Dec. 1887. CO 96/187, London CC to CO, 20 Dec. 1887.
²⁸ See Hopkins, *EcHR*, xxi, 1968, pp. 580–606. For details of the Yoruba wars during this period, see J. F. A. Ajayi and R. Smith, *Yoruba Warfare in the Nineteenth Century*, Cambridge, 1964.
²⁹ CO 879/27/345, Governor Moloney to CO, 12 May 1888; 22 May 1888. CO 879/28/355, Governor Moloney to CO, 31 May 1888, with encl.
³⁰ CO 147/64, official minutes on CO to Moloney, 31 May 1888; official minutes on Moloney to CO, 11 June 1888.
³¹ *LJC*, 5 July 1888; 12 July 1888. CO 147/64, Governor Moloney to CO, 22 May 1888. CO 879/28/355, Liverpool CC to CO, 4 July 1888; same to same, 7 July 1888.
³² *LDC*, 12 July 1888; 18 July 1888. *LJC*, 20 July 1888. *MLCC*, 19 July 1888. CO 147/68, Liverpool CC to CO, 11 July 1888; 20 July 1888.
³³ CO 147/68, official minutes on Liverpool CC to CO, 20 July 1888.
³⁴ *PMCC*, 25 July 1888.
³⁵ CO 879/28/355, Glasgow CC to CO, 23 July 1888.
³⁶ CO 879/28/355, Liverpool CC to CO, 24 July 1888.
³⁷ *LDC*, 26 July 1888.
³⁸ CO 147/68, FO to CO, 30 July 1888.
³⁹ The Colonial Office unofficially assured Governor Moloney that his treaty-making met the government's approval. CO 879/28/355, CO to Moloney, Nos. 48 and 49, 18 Oct. 1888. See also CO 876/28/355, CO to FO, 16 Oct. 1888.
⁴⁰ *LWAS*, 20 Nov. 1888.
⁴¹ *Ibid.*
⁴² CO 147/73, Liverpool CC to CO, 28 Nov. 1889 and official minutes thereon.

43 See Flint, *Goldie and the Making of Nigeria*, pp. 102–7. See also Davies, 'Sir Alfred Lewis Jones and the Development of West African Trade', pp. 73–4.

44 FO 84/1917, J. A. Baird, M.P., to FO, 9 March 1888 and official minutes thereon.

45 See *Holt Papers* (hereafter *HP*), 26/3a, John Holt to Goldie, 24 April 1888. FO 84/1925, Liverpool CC to FO, 25 July 1888. FO 84/1917, Thomas Sutherland to FO, 23 March 1888.

46 FO 84/2076, Liverpool CC to FO, 8 March 1890. See also *LDC*, 4 March 1890.

47 *MGCC*, 23 March 1886; 12 April 1886. FO/1783, Glasgow CC to FO, 10 April 1886.

48 There were financial interests in the metropolis concerned with South Africa but these were never so important as the missionary factor and they later merged with the Cape financial interests under Rhodes. See John S. Galbraith, 'Origins of the British South Africa Company', in J. Flint and G. Williams, *Perspectives of Empire*, London, 1973, pp. 148–71.

49 Cited in Anthony Dachs, 'Missionary Imperialism—the Case of Bechuanaland', *JAH*, xiii, pp. 653–4.

50 See Anthony Sillery, *John Mackenzie of Bechuanaland 1835–1899*, Cape Town, 1971, pp. 76, 119–35.

51 *Minutes of the South African Section of the London Chamber of Commerce* (hereafter *LSAS*), 30 April 1888; 14 Nov. 1888. *CCJ*, 6 Aug. 1888; 5 Sept. 1888.

52 I.e. the territory north of the South African Republic, south of the Zambezi River, east of the 20th degree of east longitude and west of the Portuguese province of Sofala. See J. Gallagher and R. Robinson, *Africa and the Victorians*, p. 222.

53 *LSAS*, 4 April 1889.

54 *MGCC*, 13 May 1889. *MBCC*, 15 May 1889. *PMCC*, 24 April 1889.

55 Gallagher and Robinson, *Africa and the Victorians*, pp. 411–15.

Seven

The recession of the early 1890s: the climax of commercial imperialism

Between about 1890 and 1894 the British economy passed through another cyclical recession. Exports slumped 16 per cent between 1890 and 1894, while gross domestic product decreased 4 per cent from 1890 to 1893 and total industrial production fell 6 per cent between 1891 and 1893.[1] Hardest hit were the iron and steel industries and the textile trades, the latter suffering also from the long-term decline in Lancashire's share of the important Indian market.

The recession brought about a great intensification of commercial pressure for intervention abroad. In its Annual Report for 1891 the Council of the Birmingham Chamber of Commerce complained of contraction in export demand, especially during the second half of that year. As business slackened, complaints became more frequent and the Reports of the Birmingham Chamber became increasingly gloomy. It was not until late 1894 that signs of improvement appeared and business confidence began to recover.[2] Since the early 1880s the Birmingham merchants took considerable interest in the debate over the desirability of a fiscal union between Britain and the colonies of settlement. The export slump of the early 1890s increased doubts about the ultimate wisdom of free trade and some Birmingham businessmen looked towards a commercial union of the Empire for a solution to Britain's economic problems. The Birmingham Chamber urged the government seriously to consider the Canadian offer of imperial preference in 1892, since 'the future prosperity of British commerce must depend on increasing our commercial relations with our Colonies'.[3] Birmingham merchants did not look only to the existing Empire: they also urged the government to open new markets for British trade in areas where there were no foreign tariffs to contend with, and they called for the extension of British influence to secure actual and potential markets in Africa and the Far East.

The directors of the Glasgow Chamber of Commerce blamed the recession on continued 'over-production'. The best remedy for this, the President of the Glasgow Chamber declared in 1892, was for British businessmen to urge the government to open up 'by railways or otherwise the countries we recently acquired in Africa and Burma'.[4] Though they were not as vocal as some of the other leading chambers of commerce, the Glasgow Chamber consistently supported overseas expansion as a remedy for economic recession in the early 1890s.

Liverpool merchants favoured a similar solution to the country's economic problems. The President of the Liverpool Chamber of Commerce pointed out in 1893 that one of the most effective remedies for the slump in business activity was 'the opening of new avenues for trade and the development of our colonial empire'.[5] Their desire to prevent the loss of potentially valuable markets behind French tariffs and to stimulate demand for British manufactures by the development of new overseas outlets led the Liverpool merchants to press strongly for extensions of British influence in Africa in the early 1890s.

It was partly because they saw the Empire as a solution to their economic problems that merchants in London advocated closer commercial relations between Britain and the settlement colonies. But the protectionist implications of schemes for a *Zollverein* or imperial preference made their acceptance difficult if not impossible because of the strength of free-trade convictions in Britain. In 1892 the London Chamber of Commerce reported: 'It is becoming more and more apparent in commercial circles . . . that there is practically no middle course for this country between a reversal of the free trade policy to which it is pledged, on the one hand, and a prudent but continuous territorial expansion for the creation of new markets on the other'.[6] New markets were to be found in Africa and Asia:

> Africa . . . presented infinite possibilities. Its peaceful partition under Lord Salisbury and its free opening to our trade was the commercial event of our century. . . . If only we would dare to govern, the development of such countries meant the renewal of trade on the grandest scale; and the same might be said of

our relations with Siam and . . . the southern provinces of China. In all this there was . . . the certainty of [economic] revival.[7]

Businessmen in Manchester became increasingly pessimistic over the prospects of trade after 1891 when the slump began to be felt in the cotton-manufacturing districts. By the beginning of 1894 things looked so black that the President of the Manchester Chamber of Commerce reported that 'most businessmen and those engaged in our great industries wished to close the book as regards 1893 and expel it from their memories'.[8] It was not until 1896 that business confidence recovered in the cotton trade. The Manchester merchants called for the development of new overseas markets to relieve the 'over-production' which they believed lay at the root of the continued economic troubles. Africa was regarded as being especially important; as the President of the Manchester Chamber said at the beginning of 1892: 'There was no doubt that Africa presented before them a field of commercial activity such as they had never known for many years, and he hoped they would take full advantage of it'.[9] During the first half of the 1890s, the Manchester merchants pressed for extensions of British territory in tropical Africa to protect free trade and to open the new markets which they believed were needed to combat the recurrent economic recessions in Britain.

The rising tide of European protectionism in the early 1890s provided additional reasons for British businessmen to seek new overseas markets. The Manchester Chamber of Commerce reported in 1894: 'It was most important that . . . they should endeavour to open up new countries under the British flag, so as to extend their trade where they could while they were being shut out by protective walls from Continental countries'.[10] The Méline tariff of 1892 signified the victory of the protectionist party in France. It confirmed the worst fears of British free-traders and dealt a shattering blow to hopes for the liberalisation of inter-European trade. Providing for increases of approximately 80 per cent over the old rates, the Méline tariff aimed at national self-sufficiency. More significantly, it marked the definite establishment of a policy of tariff assimilation of the French colonies—that is, the application of the French tariff to imports into the colonies. This policy was begun in the 1880s with the assimilation of Algeria and, to a certain extent, Indo-China into the French customs system. Tariff assimilation was now extended to include most of the French colonial possessions and showed clearly that France was determined to subordinate her colonies to the needs of the metropolitan economy.[11] The implications of this for British trade in Asia and Africa were only too obvious to British businessmen: where France succeeded in establishing her influence, British goods would be effectively excluded.

Business interest in the colonies of settlement in the early 1890s tended to focus on the colonies' value to the domestic economy. This was a significant shift from the late 1880s when the settlement empire attracted attention in the metropolis chiefly for nationalistic and sentimental reasons. While this new interest in the self-governing colonies stemmed largely from the economic recession in Britain and hostile foreign tariffs abroad, it did not produce a strong movement for commercial union of the Empire in British business circles. In fact, it had quite the opposite effect; discussion of commercial union served only to make it clear that there was no consensus among businessmen on a basis for an imperial customs union. Imperial preference, the only form of commercial unity desired by mercantile opinion in the colonies, was completely unacceptable to the majority of businessmen in the metropolis.

The most important single factor in stimulating commercial interest in the empire of settlement in the early 1890s was the sharp increase in foreign competition in neutral markets and the protectionist victories in Europe and America. The London *Chamber of Commerce Journal* called upon the government in May 1891:

> To utilize the enormous industrial and financial resources of the Mother Country for the purpose of forming a commercial partnership with the Colonies, who would bring their immense but undeveloped natural resources as their share in the partnership, and thus form a united consuming and producing community far exceeding in magnitude any recorded ancient or modern state.[12]

It was one thing to express a desire for closer commercial relations within the Empire; to formulate a definite scheme was more difficult. The Organising Committee of the London Chamber of Commerce, which set about planning the 1892 Congress of

Chambers of Commerce of the Empire, decided to solicit the views of businessmen in the metropolis and the colonies before proposing a specific plan for commercial union. The Association of U.K. Chambers of Commerce also decided in favour of some 'practical arrangement . . . to secure closer commercial union between the Mother Country and her Colonies and Dependencies'.[13] Since there were such wide differences of opinion on how closer commercial relations might be brought about, it was decided to leave the formulation of more specific proposals to the Congress of Chambers of the Empire.

From 28 June to 1 July 1892, delegates from 137 British and colonial chambers of commerce met in London. The Congress tackled some of the central commercial issues involved in the imperial relationship, touching off a debate which took up most of the time of the four-day session. There was an almost universal desire among delegates for some form of commercial union. Most British businessmen hoped to achieve commercial union by the elimination of colonial tariffs but it became evident very early in the debate that the chief colonial advocates of closer commercial relations, the Canadians, were unalterably opposed to complete free trade within the Empire. Instead, they called for a system of imperial preference in which Britain would impose a small differential duty—5 per cent was the figure most commonly suggested—against foreign imports while admitting duty-free imports from Empire countries. In return for this the Canadian delegates offered to permit British goods to enter their country at preferred rates of duty. However, these colonial proposals were flatly rejected by most British merchants.[14]

Of the major British chambers of commerce only Birmingham agreed to support imperial preference. There was unanimous agreement at the 1892 Congress on a resolution calling upon the British Government to secure the abrogation of the European treaty clauses which prevented the colonies from granting preference to the Mother Country but it was perfectly clear that on the crucial issue of commercial union the interests of colonial and British businessmen were almost diametrically opposed. In effect neither made much headway at the 1892 Congress. Towards the end of the long discussion of commercial union, one of the Canadian delegates secured an amendment to the London Chamber's resolution calling for 'free trade within the Empire' so that it read 'freer trade with the Empire', thereby losing most of its original intent.[15] The Congress indeed demonstrated the virtual impossibility of producing an imperial customs union in a form acceptable to businessmen throughout the Empire.

It was hardly surprising that with a severe slump in the cotton trade and fierce competition in world markets, Lancashire merchants and manufacturers would constantly be on the lookout for any 'unfair' advantages enjoyed by their rivals. Such an 'unfair' situation appeared to arise in 1894 when the Government of India, faced with a large budgetary deficit, imposed a general 5 per cent duty on imports. Under pressure from Lancashire cotton-manufacturing and mercantile interests, the British Government insisted that cotton goods be exempted from the duty. However, during the course of 1894, the Indian Government sought permission to extend the duties to include cotton goods. The home government agreed to this on condition that a countervailing excise duty be imposed on Indian manufactures which competed with those of Lancashire.[16]

When the Manchester Chamber of Commerce got wind of these proposals, they immediately submitted a sharp protest to the British Government. However, the strongest opposition to the new Indian duties came from various Lancashire manufacturers' associations. Their protests were particularly bitter because of the depressed conditions in the cotton trade in Britain: 'The duties had been pressed upon the Government of India by spinners and manufacturers in India. . . . The number of looms in Blackburn, Darwen, Accrington, Burnley, Church and other places which had stopped running since November was a proof how important the import duties were to these towns.'[17] Backed by the Glasgow and Manchester Chambers of Commerce and some of the smaller Lancashire chambers like Oldham and Blackburn, Lancashire manufacturers persuaded the British Government to accept most of their case against the Indian duties. Under pressure from the metropolitan government the Government of India was obliged in January 1896 to exempt cotton yarn from all taxes and to reduce the import and excise duties on cloth to $3\frac{1}{2}$ per cent.

By the early 1890s the Manchester merchants began to fear that the British Government's efforts to promote the economic development of India were having a counter-productive effect on the expansion of Indian and Far Eastern demand for British cotton manufacturers. The Indian cotton industry could not only survive; it appeared capable of competing seriously with Manchester in the markets of the Far East. As the agitation over the Indian cotton duties in 1894-5 showed, fear of Indian competition made Manchester more than ever determined to ensure that the Indian mills enjoyed no 'unnatural' advantages in their contest with Lancashire. Together with the slump in Britain and the hostile tariffs in Europe and the United States, the spectre of the loss of their valued position in the Indian market made the Manchester merchants desperately anxious to secure new overseas outlets.

The early nineties saw a quickening of commercial interest in the Far East. With the founding of the China Association in 1889, the old China hands had a powerful organisation for promoting their interests among government officials and businessmen in Britain. This, however, would not have broken the business world's apathy towards China were it not for the renewed concern over 'overproduction' in the metropolitan economy and the growing fear of foreign competition in the Far East. At the request of the China Association, metropolitan businessmen pressed the British Government to insist on stricter Chinese adherence to treaty stipulations on the movement of foreign goods and traders in the Chinese interior. The Chambers of Glasgow, Liverpool and Manchester went even further: in 1893 they supported British merchants in Hong Kong in their campaign to secure the opening of the West River to foreign steamers.[18]

Mercantile hopes for penetrating the interior markets of China focused chiefly on the construction of a direct overland route from Burma to the China frontier. The Government of India began to survey a route from Mandalay to Kunlon Ferry on the Salween River in 1892 but progress was slow, largely because of the difficult nature of the country. Meanwhile, the principal chambers of commerce pressed the government to complete the survey as soon as possible and to get on with the job of construction.[19]

Commercial pressure for the speedy completion of a trade route to the Chinese interior was intensified by French activities in Indo-China in the early 1890s. British merchants were worried by the Franco-Siamese Treaty of 1893, which was believed to embody a sinister French design to subjugate Siam. News of the agreement between France and Siam was followed by a flood of anxious inquiries to the government from the chambers of commerce, who feared that the French would obtain exclusive commercial advantages in Siam. British merchants urged their government to take steps to prevent French domination of Siam; the London and Manchester Chambers of Commerce specifically pressed for the appointment of British consular and diplomatic representatives to counter the growth of French influence in that country.[20]

What British merchants feared most of all was that unless the Burma route to south-western China was soon completed, the French would either dominate Siam and threaten Britain's 'back door' into China or tap the trade of the Chinese south-western provinces through their possessions in Tonkin. With only a few signs of improvement in the economy, the year 1895 saw a great upsurge of commercial pressure for the opening of a 'back door' into the supposedly lucrative markets of the Chinese interior.

However, it was Africa and not China that became the chief focus of commercial attention in the early 1890s. And it was Africa that was partitioned among Britain and the European powers. Throughout the first half of the 1890s British businessmen demanded that the government intervene to preserve parts of the hinterland of tropical Africa for free trade, if necessary by the extension of British rule in these regions. This 'imperialism of free trade' was seen by British merchants as a kind of anti-cyclical policy that would pull the economy out of recession by creating increased demand for exports. The course of the partition of tropical Africa in the early 1890s was largely determined by these commercial pressures in the metropolis. In West Africa the extension of British influence in the Gold Coast and what later became Nigeria followed strong mercantile pressure for intervention. Likewise in East Africa, commercial interests helped to bring intervention in Uganda. By contrast the commercial imperialism of the 1890s had little impact on southern Africa, which produced its own locally-based economic imperialism spearheaded by Cecil Rhodes.

Under the terms of the 1889 Convention between France and Britain a joint Anglo-French commission was to determine the precise boundaries of the British Colony of Sierra Leone.[21] In the meantime, however, the French pushed steadily into the West African interior from their base in Senegal. Since the trade of Sierra Leone depended to such a large extent on its position as an entrepôt for the western Sudan, the French advance alarmed British merchants and officials in the Colony. It was a British official, J. F. Parkes, Superintendent of the Aborigines Department of Sierra Leone, who brought the French movements in the hinterland to the attention of the Manchester Chamber of Commerce in July 1891. A special committee set up by the directors concluded that unless the British Government took steps to protect the Sierra Leone hinterland from French encroachment, the trade of that region would be lost entirely to France. The Manchester Chamber of Commerce reminded the Colonial Office of the 'loss of trade between this country and Sierra Leone, which is likely to arise in the event of the boundary line between the British and French spheres of influence in that region being defined so as to intercept the important caravan trade between Freetown and the interior'.[22]

Meanwhile the Liverpool merchants started to prod the Foreign Office to get on with the Sierra Leone delimitation survey, particularly in view of France's activity in West Africa. The Liverpool Chamber of Commerce regretted that the British Government had reportedly agreed to French claims north of the Mellacourie River and expressed concern 'lest further concessions calculated to injure them . . . should be made to the French'. The Liverpool merchants urged that

> steps should immediately be taken to protect the interests of British commerce in the countries adjacent to Sierra Leone which are still free from foreign European control . . . unless freedom of trade in the interior is secured either by treaty or by the establishment of British spheres of influence, the Colonies of the Coast must ultimately become useless for commerce.[23]

They specifically urged the government to accept the offer of Samori to place his extensive kingdom under British protection. Since the bulk of Sierra Leone's trade with the interior passed through this powerful African state, such a policy would safeguard free trade in that region. The Liverpool merchants invited the other major chambers of commerce to join their deputation to the Foreign Office to press these views upon the British Government. The Glasgow Chamber promised to support Liverpool and reminded the Foreign Office of the importance of securing free access to the interior. Meanwhile, the Chambers of Commerce of Birmingham, Glasgow, London and Manchester agreed to join the Liverpool deputation to the Foreign Office.[24]

However, unknown to the metropolitan businessmen, the Anglo-French agreement of 1889 had in fact already settled respective spheres of influence around Sierra Leone and had *inter alia* accepted an 1882 Convention recognising French claims north of the Mellacourie River. Moreover, the British Government had accepted France's declaration of a protectorate over Samori's empire in 1887.[25] The mercantile pressure over Sierra Leone at the end of 1891 was highly embarrassing to the Foreign Office, for it appeared that it might be accused of having thrown overboard the interests of British trade with West Africa. Neither the Colonial Office nor the Foreign Office welcomed this prospect and neither wished to accept responsibility for the concessions to France in the region of Sierra Leone. The Chambers' deputation originally proposed to meet the Foreign Secretary, Lord Salisbury, but the government subsequently arranged that Lord Knutsford, the Secretary of State for the Colonies, should receive them.[26] Accordingly on 8 December 1891 the deputation, representing the Chambers of Commerce of Birmingham, Glasgow, Liverpool, London and Manchester, interviewed the Colonial Secretary.

Knutsford's revelation of France's gains in the Sierra Leone area was a bombshell for the merchants, since they were totally unaware of the extent to which the British Government had accepted French claims in that region.[27] In defending the government, Knutsford told the merchants that the Salisbury administration upon entering office found that a convention had been in effect since 1882 by which the Northern Rivers were recognised as French territory; though never officially ratified, the agreement had been subsequently accepted as binding by both governments. As for Samori's territory, the Colonial Secretary argued that nothing had been surrendered in 1889, since Samori had placed all his territories under French protection by a treaty of 1887.[28]

Knutsford's explanations failed to satisfy the Liverpool merchants. The President of the Liverpool Chamber of Commerce indignantly charged that while the West African trade 'had been made by British merchants, the Government had supinely allowed foreigners to wedge themselves into different parts of the coast and especially to attack the Hinterland [sic] upon which the growth and continuation of trade depended'.[29] On 18 December the Liverpool Chamber of Commerce expressed its feeling of 'astonishment and regret' at the announcement of the Colonial Secretary. Liverpool merchants accused the government of neglecting the commercial interests of the nation. The *Liverpool Mercury* wrote on 19 December 1891: 'The question of the West African hinterland was a national one, viewed in the light of the employment the trade gave to British merchants, shipowners, manufacturers and artisans'.[30] The reactions of the other major chambers were more restrained. While they regretted the outcome of the government's policy in Sierra Leone, they accepted the Colonial Secretary's explanations and there was no general commercial campaign to undo the Anglo-French agreement. The directors of the Manchester Chamber of Commerce expressed great dissatisfaction with the Sierra Leone settlement but decided to leave the subject in the hands of Liverpool.[31] The directors of the Glasgow Chamber were likewise unwilling to pursue the Sierra Leone boundary question any further at that time.[32] Although the London merchants were unhappy at the outcome, they did no more than ask the government to examine the political claims of the French treaties.[33] Since there was little likelihood of a general commercial agitation, the government refused to re-open the Sierra Leone boundary question.[34]

The Anglo-French settlement of the boundaries of Sierra Leone has been cited as proof of the irrelevance of British commercial pressures to the partition of West Africa.[35] But this judgement will not bear close scrutiny. The Anglo-French Convention of 1889 was uninfluenced by mercantile concerns because commercial interests at that time made no serious attempts to exert pressure on the government. Despite the clamour of the Sierra Leone merchants, the chambers of commerce, unaware of the actual extent of the concessions gained by the French, did not move in 1889 and, with economic activity on the upswing, the pressures for expansion were temporarily lessened. When they learned at the end of 1891 of the extent of France's gains in the neighbourhood of Sierra Leone, British merchants were taken completely by surprise. However, business opinion in general was prepared to accept the Sierra Leone settlement as a *fait accompli* and there was no commercial agitation for reopening the question.

Nonetheless the revelation of France's gains in the Sierra Leone region at the end of 1891 marked a significant turning point in the partition of West Africa. Coinciding as it did with the beginnings of another slump in British exports and news of the Méline tariff in France, it produced a sharp outcry in commercial circles. If there was nothing to be done to recover what had been 'lost' in the area of Sierra Leone, the principal chambers of commerce were determined that the Sierra Leone experience would not be repeated elsewhere in West Africa. A commercial campaign to extend British influence into the West African interior developed at the beginning of 1892.

In Liverpool there were hundreds of manufacturers and merchants interested in the West African trade and anger at the government's weakness and failure to protect British commerce was very widespread. As one Liverpool manufacturer put it, Liverpool businessmen felt 'that markets which they are entitled to look upon as a yearly increasing outlet for home manufactures are being quietly handed over to the French without due consideration on the part of Her Majesty's Government'.[36] The Liverpool Chamber of Commerce demanded 'that British interests should be secured in the territories of West Africa where British trade predominates, and which are unappropriated by any European power, by arranging that such territories shall be spheres of British influence'.[37]

At the same time commercial opinion in Manchester began to mobilise. On 20 January 1892 a deputation of African merchants presented a petition to the Board of Directors of the Manchester Chamber of Commerce signed by more than ninety Manchester firms and individual merchants proposing the formation of an African Trade Section.[38] African merchants in Manchester pointed out that the recent 'startling disclosures' of French activity in the region of Sierra Leone necessitated strong action by the government if Britain was not to lose potentially valuable markets behind French tariffs as in Senegal, Algeria and other French colonies. The Manchester Chamber of Commerce urged the Colonial Office to take 'immediate steps to prevent further alienation by any foreign power of territory in the hinterland of West Africa with which British trade is carried on directly or indirectly'.[39] At the beginning of March the Manchester Chamber set up an African Sectional Committee which immediately began to push vigorously for the extension of British rule throughout West Africa.

During the early months of 1892 pressure for a strong imperial policy in West Africa came from commercial groups throughout the country. In February the Council of the Birmingham Chamber requested the Colonial Office to instruct Governors in the West

African Colonies to make treaties with African chiefs in the hinterlands of British possessions to ensure that their territories would
not be placed under the exclusive protection of any but British rule
or 'otherwise to secure the Hinterlands'.[40] In the same month the
directors of the Glasgow Chamber of Commerce urged the Colonial
Office to negotiate treaties with chiefs in the hinterlands of Britain's
West African possessions.[41] In March the Council of the London
Chamber pressed the Colonial Office for the extension of British
influence in the interior of the Gold Coast and Lagos.[42] This commercial pressure played a key role in the British interventions in
the territories that later became Ghana and Nigeria and in the
interlacustrine region of East Africa.

The British position in the hinterland of the Gold Coast was
highly fluid in the early 1890s, since the Anglo-French Convention
of 1889 defined the western boundary of the British protectorate
for only twenty miles inland and the French were known to be
active in the Gold Coast interior.[43] In the commercial agitation
following the revelation of the government's 'surrender' in Sierra
Leone, the London Chamber of Commerce focused its attention
chiefly on the Gold Coast, where the African merchants of the City
did a large proportion of their trade. The London merchants
clamoured for the extension of British influence to the territory
north of the ninth parallel of latitude.[44] Under heavy pressure to
protect British trade in West Africa, the government could not
afford to let the Gold Coast go the way of Sierra Leone. In March
1892 Lord Salisbury decided that '... it would ... be advisable to
anticipate French agents by the conclusion of treaties' with the
chiefs of Dagomba, Gondja, Mossi and Gourounsi in the Gold
Coast hinterland, a decision which was communicated confiden-
tially to the executive of the London Chamber's West African
Trade Section.[45] The Gold Coast Government accordingly
despatched an agent, George Ferguson, who concluded a series of
treaties with the more important northern tribes of the Gold Coast
by which the chiefs agreed not to accept the protection of any
Power without British consent. Although not all of these treaties
were subsequently upheld, Ferguson's mission showed clearly that
the government was determined to secure as much as possible of
the Gold Coast interior for British commerce.[46]

While the British Government, in response to mercantile pressure, extended its influence north of Ashanti, it was still reluctant

to intervene directly in the affairs of Ashanti itself. Towards the end of 1893 a number of Glasgow merchants in the Gold Coast trade wrote to the Colonial Office urging the extension of British protection to Ashanti. At the beginning of 1894 the directors of the Glasgow Chamber of Commerce pointed out to the Colonial Office that the cost of taking over and administering Ashanti would be repaid by the increased revenue from that region if it was placed under British rule.[47] The Liverpool and London Chambers of Commerce also pressed the government to extend protection to Ashanti.[48] Although the directors of the Manchester Chamber did not ask the government for intervention in Ashanti, they agreed to join any deputation to the Colonial Office on that subject.[49]

Brandford Griffith, the Gold Coast Governor, agreed with the merchants on the need for intervention, but the Colonial Secretary, Lord Ripon, was opposed, believing that the time was not yet ripe for such a step.[50] During 1894 the Liverpool Chamber repeatedly pressed the Colonial Office to appoint a British Resident at Kumasi, the Ashanti capital. The Colonial Office insisted that since France was safely excluded from Ashanti by the 1889 agreement, there was no need for any direct British presence. This argument failed to convince the merchants and the commercial pressure intensified in 1895. Arguing that Ashanti was hindering the growth of British trade with the interior, the Chambers of Glasgow, Liverpool, London and Manchester bombarded the government with demands for intervention.[51] Some of the permanent officials at the Colonial Office accepted the case for intervention at the beginning of 1895, as did the new Governor, Sir William Maxwell, who took up his post in March.[52] All that was required now was the sanction of government ministers at home. The decision to send an ultimatum to the King of Ashanti, requiring him to accept a British Resident at Kumasi, was made by Ripon's successor at the Colonial Office, Joseph Chamberlain, in September 1895. The new Colonial Secretary's policy of pegging out claims for the future of British trade was exactly what metropolitan mercantile interests were calling for.

As in the Gold Coast, the British position in the Lagos hinterlands was precarious at the beginning of the 1890s. The Anglo-French agreement of 1889 did not preclude the possibility that the French would move into Yorubaland from north of the ninth parallel. The British Government itself showed no intention of becoming involved in the affairs of Yorubaland, despite the clamour of the Lagos merchants, who wanted British intervention as a means of ending the protracted internecine struggles among the Yoruba.

At the request of merchants in Lagos in 1891, the Chambers of Commerce of Liverpool and Manchester asked the Colonial Office to mediate a peace settlement between rival Yoruba states and to negotiate with Yoruba authorities for the abolition of tolls levied on goods passing through their territories.[53] In response to these pressures, the Colonial Office instructed Acting Governor Denton to make an official tour of the hinterland to mediate a peace settlement. However, neither Denton nor Carter, the new Governor, was able to negotiate a permanent peace between the two chief Yoruba rivals, the Egba and the Ijebu. Worse still for the Lagos merchants, the Egba and the Ijebu sunk their differences, at least for the moment, and closed the trade routes to Lagos in February 1892.[54]

The Colonial Office, already under heavy pressure from the chambers of commerce, was now flooded with demands for action in Yorubaland. On 17 February 1892 the Liverpool merchants pressed the government for immediate action to secure the reopening of the Lagos roads to the interior. In March African merchants in Manchester and Liverpool held a conference with prominent Lancashire M.P.s and stressed the importance of reopening the trade routes in Yorubaland, arguing that coercion ought to be used if necessary. The same month the directors of the Manchester Chamber of Commerce pressed the government to obtain a 'permanent' settlement of the Lagos roads problem. Meanwhile, the Liverpool Chamber bombarded the Colonial Office for information on the steps it proposed to take to reopen the trade routes.[55]

By March 1892 the mercantile agitation was beginning to bear fruit and the Governor of Lagos was informed that the Colonial Office was considering coercion of the Ijebu.[56] Under growing mercantile pressure, the government gave way and in May preparations were made for an expedition against the Ijebu, whose speedy defeat by British forces the same month was followed by demands from the Liverpool merchants for similar action against the Egba. This proved unnecessary since the Egba, perhaps influenced by the defeat of the Ijebu, agreed to open their trade routes later in the year. The results of the government's forceful action in Yorubaland were greeted with jubilation by the Lancashire merchants.[57]

In 1893 the Egba and the Ijebu submitted to treaties ending the conflict in Yorubaland and guaranteeing freedom of movement for traders. Although the legal status of these territories remained unaltered, both were now virtually under the control of the Governor of Lagos. The forceful assertion of British authority in 1892 proved decisive for the rest of Yorubaland. The breach had been made and the subsequent conclusion of a network of treaties brought the whole of Yorubaland under British influence by 1896.

Although the government proclaimed the Niger Coast Protectorate, following the mercantile campaign against chartered company rule for the delta region in 1891, it was slow to define the boundaries between the Protectorate and the territories of the Royal Niger Company. Meanwhile the Niger Company took advantage of the delay to extend its influence into the coastal regions of the Niger delta before the new protectorate administration could settle its boundaries. The African Section of the Liverpool Chamber of Commerce, supported by the shipping companies, the African Association and the commission houses, protested vigorously to the Foreign Office. The Liverpool merchants argued that the Niger Company's sphere of influence should be restricted to the Upper Niger and Benue and that the whole of the delta should come under the new protectorate. But the Foreign Office somewhat disingenuously replied that such a step would be an infringement of the Niger Company's charter.[58]

The Liverpool merchants then tried to negotiate directly with the Royal Niger Company. Against the background of a bitter trade war on the Niger between Liverpool merchants and the chartered company, the African Trade Section of the Liverpool Chamber arranged a conference with Goldie in December 1892. The Liverpool merchants presented a set of proposals for basic reforms in the Niger Company, which would have forced the latter to forego its monopolistic position. Assured of the government's support, however, the Niger Company refused to co-operate with the Liverpool merchants and the negotiations quickly broke down.[59]

Not content merely to beat off attacks by its opponents, the Niger Company fought back. By a series of shrewd political manœuvres it succeeded in disarming most of its mercantile critics in Britain and frustrating what might have developed into a major attack on its own charter. That it was able to retain the charter despite growing mercantile hostility in Britain to the whole chartered company idea was largely due to its successful counter-attack. Liverpool's campaign against the Niger Company suffered a setback in March 1893 when A. L. Jones resigned his chairmanship of the African Trade Section of the Liverpool Chamber. Jones had led the shipping interests in the battle against the company but when Goldie offered Elder Dempster Lines a long-term contract early in 1893, Jones was persuaded to drop his opposition to the Niger Company.[60] However, this did not lessen the Liverpool Chamber's attacks on the company; John Holt, the new Vice-Chairman of the African Trade Section, denounced the 'brazen wall of monopoly' of the Niger Company in March 1893 and the Liverpool Chamber of Commerce continued to press the government for reforms which would guarantee complete freedom of trade on the Niger. At the annual meeting of the Liverpool Chamber in April 1893, the President of the Chamber called for basic reforms in the Niger Company 'in the interests alike of Free Trade and of the natives of its territories'.[61] Opposition to the Niger Company was further weakened in June 1893 when the African Association reached an agreement with the company for the fusion of their interests on the Niger. Frustrated by their lack of success against the company, the Liverpool Chamber now began to call for the revocation of the Royal Charter. The government was, however, fully aware of the differences of opinion among Liverpool merchants and it turned a deaf ear to these demands.[62]

The Liverpool merchants were unable to win support from the other major chambers of commerce in their attack on the Niger Company. Dominated by its colourful Chairman, George Goldie, the West African Section of the London Chamber of Commerce assiduously avoided all discussion of the Royal Niger Company. The Liverpool merchants approached the Glasgow Chamber in 1893 but the latter felt 'insufficiently acquainted with the facts' of the Niger situation to form an opinion for or against the Niger Company.[63] Since cotton textiles figured so prominently in British exports to West Africa, the attitude of the Manchester Chamber of Commerce was bound to carry considerable weight. But the Royal Niger Company shrewdly removed all duties on imports of cotton goods into its territories, which partly accounted for Manchester's silence. Moreover, the Chairman of the

Manchester Chamber's African Sectional Committee, James Hutton, was a shareholder in the Royal Niger Company. Several times during 1893 Manchester was approached by individual African merchants and by the Liverpool Chamber but on each occasion the Manchester Chamber postponed discussion of the Niger Company. The subject was finally adjourned *sine die*.[64] It was not until the middle of 1894, when the Liverpool merchants began to press for a customs union between the territories of the Royal Niger Company and the Niger Coast Protectorate, that they received any support from the other chambers on the Niger question. As long as opposition to the Niger Company was restricted to Liverpool, the government was able to ignore it. Had the full weight of commercial opinion in the country mobilised itself against the Niger Company's Charter, there is little doubt that the outcome would have been different.

It was not long, however, before complaints against the Niger Company came from other quarters. Towards the end of 1894 the company's exclusive policy in the Oil Rivers provoked an armed assault on its Niger headquarters by Africans from the nearby town of Brass. The Liverpool Chamber of Commerce triumphantly proclaimed that the attack was damning proof of the iniquity of the company's rule and a conclusive demonstration that the trade of the delta could only be satisfactorily developed by a customs union of the territories of the Niger Company and the Niger Coast Protectorate.[65] While not committing themselves to any judgement of the responsibility for the attack on the Niger Company, the Manchester Chamber supported Liverpool's demands for the despatch of a special commissioner to inquire into the affair and to consider the possibility of a customs union.[66] Although none of the other major chambers of commerce took up the issue of a customs union at that time, the year 1895 marked the beginning of a series of sharp attacks on the Niger Company by metropolitan businessmen. The growing hostility towards chartered companies was shared by Joseph Chamberlain, who became Colonial Secretary in September 1895. The Niger Company was to keep its charter for another five years but its days were already numbered, and after 1895 its influence in both official and unofficial circles underwent a steady decline.

Despite their momentous significance for the future of the Empire, events in southern Africa attracted only peripheral attention from British commercial opinion in the early 1890s. In 1892 the South African Section of the London Chamber of Commerce resolved to extend its 'moral support' to a scheme for the construction of a railway from Swaziland to the ocean.[67] While the Birmingham and Liverpool Chambers supported the general idea of government assistance in providing such a railway, the directors of the Glasgow Chamber of Commerce felt that no special urging was needed, for the government was sufficiently sympathetic to 'judicious enterprise' in any case.[68] The directors of the Manchester Chamber, on the other hand, flatly refused to support the Swaziland railway.[69]

In fact the British Government was about to hand Swaziland over to the South African Republic as part of its policy of cajoling the Boers into a commercial union with the Cape Colony. The London Chamber was strongly opposed to such a course[70] and for a moment it looked as if there might be a general commercial protest. The Birmingham Chamber denounced the 'handing over' of Swaziland to the Boers but commercial opinion in general did not take up the issue. Businessmen appeared to accept the Foreign Office's assurances that British commercial interests in Swaziland would be adequately protected in the transfer.[71]

The early 1890s saw considerable commercial pressure for direct intervention in the interlacustrine region of East Africa. A few British missionaries and traders had been active in Buganda and its neighbouring region in the 1880s. By the Anglo-German agreement of 1890 Germany accepted *inter alia* British claims to a sphere of influence which included Buganda. The British government hoped that Mackinnon's East Africa Company, chartered in 1888 and already working towards the interior, would be able to undertake the job of asserting British influence in Uganda. Mackinnon's company lacked the resources for such a task, however, and at the end of 1891 ordered its agents to withdraw from Uganda to the coast.[72] Meanwhile the Church Missionary Society scraped together sufficient funds to reach an agreement with the company for the postponement of evacuation for one year. This was a stopgap measure only and Mackinnon announced that his company could not possibly remain in Uganda beyond the end of 1892.[73] When, towards the end of 1892, supporters of Mackinnon appealed to the British public to prevent a withdrawal from Uganda, they received vigorous backing from commercial opinion throughout

Britain. Uganda was seen in business circles as another potentially valuable market that should remain open to free trade. If its development could not be safely entrusted to a chartered company, then the British Government should administer it directly. With the British economy in trouble the abandonment of potential markets to Britain's commercial rivals would be unthinkable.

On 16 November 1892 the Council of the Birmingham Chamber of Commerce unanimously resolved that 'in view of the depressed state of trade', Her Majesty's Government should be urged to retain Uganda under British influence. After hearing an address by Captain Lugard at a special meeting on 2 December, the Birmingham merchants again wrote to the Foreign Office on Uganda, pointing out 'the advantages that it offers for the extension of British commerce' and urging its retention under British rule.[74] In response to appeals from the British East Africa Company at the beginning of November, the directors of the Glasgow Chamber of Commerce informed the Foreign Office of the likelihood of a revival of the slave trade should Britain withdraw from Uganda, and they reminded the government of the great value of the country for the future of British commerce.[75] On 30 November a special meeting of the Liverpool Chamber of Commerce resolved to petition the government to retain Uganda. However, partly because of their strong antipathy towards the Niger Company, many of the African merchants of Liverpool urged the government to bring Uganda directly under British administration.[76] After hearing an address by Captain Lugard on the commercial possibilities of Uganda, the London Chamber of Commerce warned the Foreign Office against the abandonment of 'such a fruitful and promising territory, and one which is of such vital importance to our position in Africa'.[77] The President of the Manchester Chamber said in November: 'With a falling off of British exports amounting to 9 per cent in the first nine months of the year as compared with last year, they certainly wanted new markets. It was with this object that they invited Captain Lugard to address the meeting [on Uganda]'.[78] Since they hesitated at the idea of advocating government aid for a chartered company, the Manchester directors asked the Foreign Office that Uganda be retained directly by the government and that 'any steps taken for opening up of the country be based on the assumption by Her Majesty's Government of the administration of the whole territory from the coast to the interior'.[79]

Towards the end of 1892 there was massive pressure on the British Government to retain Uganda. In November and December resolutions urging retention came from the Chambers of Commerce of Blackburn, Dewsbury, Dundee, Edinburgh, Exeter, Gloucester, Greenock, Leeds, Leith, Middlesbrough, Newport, Rochdale, Southampton, Stockton-on-Tees, Swansea, Walsall and Worcester.[80] During these months the government came under great pressure from missionary and humanitarian groups throughout the country, many of whom also stressed the value of Uganda for the future expansion of British trade and industry.[81] It would be impossible to isolate the effects of mercantile pressure in the public campaign for the retention of Uganda at the end of 1892. It is certain, however, that the public pressure was a major factor in the government's decision in favour of retention. It is equally certain that British businessmen were highly satisfied with the outcome. When the Cabinet's decision against evacuation was formally announced, it was enthusiastically applauded in the major commercial and industrial centres because of the expected benefits to British trade. The *Chamber of Commerce Journal* commented: 'We have never ceased to urge the paramount importance to British trade of availing ourselves of every opportunity for expansion, and the creation of fresh markets, and, if we may judge from all received accounts, East Africa is one of very great potentialities.'[82] The President of the Manchester Chamber of Commerce told the members that they could

> congratulate themselves on the fact that the Government had made up its mind to administer Uganda. (Hear, hear.) That would be a good acquisition. . . . It was most important that in this way they should endeavour to open up new countries under the British flag, so as to extend their trade where they could while they were being shut out by protective tariffs from Continental countries.[83]

In a circular to local M.P.s, the Council of the Birmingham Chamber of Commerce declared that 'the great hope inspired by the acquisition of our East African territories was the opening of new markets where our trade would be unhampered by hostile tariffs which confront it almost everywhere else'.[84] The promotion of free trade abroad and the restoration of prosperity at home seemed to be inextricably bound up with imperial expansion.

Notes

1. Calculated from Feinstein, *National Income, Expenditure and Output of the United Kingdom 1855–1965*, Table 3, col. 2; Table 4, col. 5; Table 51, col. 1.
2. See *RBCC*, 1892–6.
3. *RBCC*, 1893.
4. *AMGC*, 18 Jan. 1892.
5. *LJC*, 8 April 1893.
6. *LCCR*, 1892.
7. *CCJ*, June 1894.
8. *MG*, 6 Feb. 1894.
9. *MG*, 2 Feb. 1892.
10. *MG*, 8 May 1894.
11. See Clough, *France. A History of National Economics*, pp. 225–9, and Girault, *Colonial Tariff Policy*, p. 81ff.
12. *CCJ*, 11 May 1891.
13. *CCJ*, 10 Sept. 1891.
14. See *Proceedings of the Second Congress of Chambers of Commerce of the Empire, 1892*, London, 1892.
15. *Ibid.*
16. See Peter Harnetty, 'The Indian Cotton Duties Controversy, 1894–1896', *English Historical Review*, lxxvii, Oct. 1962, pp. 684–702.
17. *MG*, 5 Feb. 1895.
18. *PMCC*, 26 Oct. 1893. *MGCC*, 13 Nov. 1893. *RLCC*, 1894.
19. See, for examples, *MBCC*, 10 Aug. 1891. *PMCC*, 22 July 1891. *MLCC*, 30 Sept. 1891. *MGCC*, 12 Oct. 1891.
20. See *PMCC*, 27 Sept. 1893; 5 Oct. 1893. *MGCC*, 10 Oct. 1893. *LJC*, 30 Oct. 1893. *RBCC*, 1894. *CCJ*, May 1894 Supp.
21. See above, pp. 96–102.
22. CO 267/392, Manchester CC to CO, 24 Nov. 1891.
23. FO 84/2179, Liverpool CC to FO, 18 Nov. 1891.
24. CO 267/392, Liverpool CC to CO, 5 Nov. 1891.
25. See official minutes on CO 267/392, Liverpool CC to CO, 18 Nov. 1891 and official minutes on Manchester CC to CO, 24 Nov. 1891.
26. See Minuet by Hemming on CO 267/398, FO to CO, 26 May 1892.
27. See, for examples, *LJC*, 9 Feb. 1892. *LWAS*, 24 Feb. 1892. *PMCC*, 30 May 1892. *RACC*, Oct. 1892.

28 CO 267/397, Liverpool CC to CO, 18 Jan. 1891 with enclosures.
29 *LJC*, 9 Dec. 1891.
30 Encl. in CO 267/392, Liverpool CC to CO, 18 Dec. 1891.
31 *PMCC*, 16 Dec. 1891.
32 *MGCC*, 14 Dec. 1891; 11 Jan. 1892; 8 Feb. 1892.
33 FO 82/2244, London CC to CO, 8 March 1892.
34 CO 267/398, FO to CO, 17 March 1892, encl. of draft letter to Liverpool CC. Minutes and encls. in CO 267/398, FO to CO, 19 May 1892; same to same, 13 July 1892. CO 267/396, official minutes on Governor Fleming to CO, 22 Oct. 1892.
35 Gallagher and Robinson, *Africa and the Victorians*, pp. 382–3.
36 *LJC*, 2 Feb. 1892.
37 CO 267/397, Liverpool CC to CO, 26 Feb. 1892, and encls.
38 *PMCC*, 20 Jan. 1892.
39 *PMCC*, 10 Feb. 1892.
40 *MBCC*, 17 Feb. 1892. CO 147/88, Birmingham CC to CO, 18 Feb. 1892.
41 CO 147/88, Glasgow CC to CO, 23 Feb. 1892.
42 *LWAS*, 24 Feb. 1892. CO 96/228, London CC to CO, 5 March 1892; same to same, 8 March 1892.
43 See Kimble, *Political History of Ghana*, p. 279, and R. E. Dummett, 'British Official Attitudes in Relation to Economic Development in the Gold Coast, 1874–1905'. Ph.D. thesis, London, 1966, p. 159.
44 *LWAS*, 24 Feb. 1892. CO 96/228, London CC to CO, 5 March 1892; 8 March 1892.
45 CO 879/38/448, FO to CO, 24 March 1892.
46 See Dummett, 'British Official Attitudes', pp. 170–1.
47 *MGCC*, 8 Jan. 1894; 22 Jan. 1894. CO 96/250, Glasgow CC to CO, 26 Jan. 1894.
48 *LJC*, 8 Jan. 1894; 27 Jan. 1894. *LWAS*, 12 Dec. 1893. *Minutes of the Council of the London Chamber of Commerce* (hereafter *LCCM*, 11 Jan. 1894. CO 96/250, London CC to CO, 13 Jan. 1894.
49 *Minutes of the African Sectional Committee of the Manchester Chamber of Commerce* (hereafter *MASEC*), 10 Jan. 1894; 13 March 1894. *PMCC*, 14 March 1894.
50 CO 96/248, Griffith to CO, 28 Sept. 1894 and minute by Ripon.
51 *MGCC*, 11 Feb. 1895; 8 April 1895; 12 Aug. 1895. CO 96/266, Glasgow CC to CO, 14 March 1895; same to same, 14 Sept,

1895. *LJC*, 5 Feb. 1895; 16 Feb. 1895. CO 96/266, Liverpool CC to CO, 18 May 1895; 6 Aug. 1895; 26 Aug. 1895; 25 Sept. 1895. *LWAS*, 23 Jan. 1895; 21 June 1895; 1 Aug. 1895. CO 96/266, London CC to CO, 26 Jan. 1895; same to same, 3 Aug. 1895; same to same, 28 Aug. 1895. *MASEC*, 6 Feb. 1895; 31 July 1895. CO 96/266, Manchester CC to CO, 15 Feb. 1895; same to same, 11 May 1895; same to same, 5 Oct. 1895.

[52] See A. W. L. Hemming's minute on CO 96/266, Liverpool CC to CO, 20 Feb. 1895. See also Kimble, *Political History of Ghana*, pp. 288–90.

[53] *LJC*, 24 March 1891. *MLCC*, 3 April 1891. *PMCC*, 25 March 1891. CO 147/83, Liverpool CC to CO, 6 April 1891; Manchester CC to CO, 31 March 1891.

[54] For an excellent detailed account of the background to these events, see A. G. Hopkins, 'Economic Imperialism in West Africa: Lagos, 1880–92', *EcHR*, 2nd ser., xxi, 1968, pp. 580–606.

[55] See CO 147/88, Liverpool CC to CO, 17 Feb. 1892; 9 March 1892; 12 March 1892; 14 March 1892; 21 March 1892: Manchester CC to CO, 9 March 1892.

[56] CO 147/84, official minutes on Carter to CO, 10 March 1892 and official minutes on same to same (tel.), 16 March 1892.

[57] See Hopkins, *EcHR*, xxi, p. 602.

[58] See Flint, *Sir George Goldie*, p. 188.

[59] *LJC*, 16 Jan. 1893. FO 84/2266, Royal Niger Co. to CO, 19 Dec. 1892. See also Flint, *Goldie*, pp. 195–6.

[60] *LJC*, 8 March 1893. Davies, 'Sir Alfred Lewis Jones', pp. 92–3.

[61] *LJC*, 8 April 1893.

[62] FO 83/1238, FO to Liverpool CC, 14 April 1893. *LJC*, 29 July 1893. FO 83/1241, Liverpool CC to FO, 28 July 1893. FO 84/2256, memo. by Anderson, Aug. 1892.

[63] *MGCC*, 14 Aug. 1893.

[64] *MASEC*, 7 June 1893; 5 July 1893; 22 Aug. 1893.

[65] FO 83/1375, Liverpool CC to CO, 14 Feb. 1895.

[66] FO 83/1376, Manchester CC to CO, 14 March 1895.

[67] *LSAS*, 11 April 1892. *LCCM*, 12 April 1892.

[68] *MBCC*, 18 May 1892. *LJC*, 26 May 1892; 15 June 1892. *MLCC*, 25 May 1892; 13 July 1892. *MGCC*, 9 May 1892; 13 June 1892; 12 Nov. 1892.

[69] *PMCC*, 18 May 1892.

[70] *RLCC*, 1892.

[71] *MBCC*, 1 Jan. 1893. *MGCC*, 10 April 1893; 25 April 1893; 15 Nov. 1894.

[72] Anthony Low, 'British Public Opinion and the Uganda Question: October and December, 1892', *Uganda Journal*, 1954, p. 81. See also Galbraith, *Mackinnon and East Africa*, p. 198.

[73] Low, *Uganda Journal*, 1954, 82.

[74] *MBCC*, 16 Nov. 1892. FO 84/2192, Birmingham CC to FO, 16 Nov. 1892; 3 Dec. 1892.

[75] *MGCC*, 2 Nov. 1892. FO 84/2192, Glasgow CC to FO, 2 Nov. 1892.

[76] *LJC*, 1 Dec. 1892. *MLCC*, 6 Dec. 1892; 14 Dec. 1892. FO 84/2192, Liverpool CC to FO, 7 Dec. 1892.

[77] *LCCM*, 10 Nov. 1892. FO 84/2192, London CC to FO, 7 Dec. 1892.

[78] *MG*, 8 Nov. 1892.

[79] *PMCC*, 14 Nov. 1892. FO 84/2192, Manchester CC to FO, 14 Nov. 1892.

[80] All filed in FO 84/2192.

[81] See Low, *Uganda Journal*, 1954, 81–100.

[82] *CCJ*, April 1894.

[83] *MG*, 8 May 1894.

[84] *RBCC*, 1894.

Eight

Conclusion: business recession and imperial expansion

While businessmen were generally in favour of extending British overseas trade, they felt no compelling need for new markets or sources of supply in the early 1870s. In any case it was to the traditional European and North American markets and not to distant tropical regions that they primarily looked for increased trade. Still less were they prepared to advocate government intervention in distant non-colonial regions. With a business boom at home and a buoyant demand for British goods in the 'civilised' markets of the world in these years, areas of low consuming power like Africa and the Far East held few attractions for British trade and industry. Free trade appeared to have struck firm roots in the more 'enlightened' nations of western Europe. Moreover, free-trade theory and practice provided strong arguments against meddling in other people's affairs, particularly in the case of 'savage' African tribesmen and 'corrupt' Chinese mandarins. While British commercial opinion was not prepared to accept the abandonment of existing imperial commitments, it would not support proposals for the extension of British power and influence in Africa and Asia.

Although European procrastination over tariff reductions and the recession in the British economy in the late 1870s dampened hopes for the rapid attainment of universal free trade, British merchants did not lose their faith in the ultimate triumph of that principle. To be sure, there were signs of a protectionist revival in Europe in the late 1880s but commercial opinion in Britain was still optimistic over the future of free trade on the Continent. While the recession of 1875–9 had severe effects on some sections of trade and industry, recovery set in before any substantial segment of the business community strayed from economic orthodoxy. Nor did the recession stimulate any great interest in expansion abroad. Despite the slump, few British businessmen turned to the colonies of settlement, India or imperial expansion in Africa and Asia for solutions to their economic problems. The only exception to this occurred in Lancashire, where the severity of the slump produced the first signs of the new commercial imperialism that was to become so prominent in the next two decades. At the beginning of 1879 there was considerable interest in Lancashire commercial circles in the idea of opening a new market in Central Africa as a solution to the slump in the British economy. Because this new commercial interest in Africa was so closely linked to business conditions in the metropolis, it did not survive the upswing in economic activity that occurred in the second half of 1879.

A severe economic slump in the mid 1880s gave rise to a widespread belief in commercial circles that the economy was suffering from 'over-production'. Businessmen turned increasingly towards the idea of expanding demand by the opening of new export markets in undeveloped or hitherto neglected areas of the world. Such an approach was regarded as perfectly compatible with free trade doctrine. Around the same time, commercial opinion began to demand increased government support for overseas trade. The prevailing economic slump and the assistance given by foreign governments to their merchants and industrialists made it seem less likely that individual enterprise in Britain would receive its just reward without the help of government. It was no accident, however, that the strongest demands for state aid to business were invoked in the sphere of overseas trade. Because of the gold standard, monetary policy was believed to be beyond the control of government; the state could exercise no stabilising influence on the economy through this medium. The British Government lacked the will to formulate a national economic policy or the institutions and capacity to execute such a policy. The prevailing free-trade ideology of British business and officialdom precluded a national strategy of protecting the home market. Thus overseas trade was almost the only sphere wherein a state-directed anti-cyclical policy could operate.

Few businessmen turned to the settlement colonies for new overseas markets. They looked instead to the opening of hitherto unexploited regions in Africa and Asia. The south-west provinces of China appeared to offer a vast market provided suitable communications could be constructed. French competition and hostile French tariffs threatened to cut off British trade with Indo-China and French expansion in south-east Asia could put Britain's Gallic rival in a position to tap the trade of the Chinese interior through Tonkin; private enterprise in Britain could not be expected to compete with the state-sponsored trade of the French unless it received government assistance. Leading British chambers of commerce therefore urged Her Majesty's Government to assist in the construction of a railway from Burma to the Chinese border. Upper Burma was not only part of the 'highway to China' but, as the Rangoon merchants pointed out, a potentially valuable market in its own right. If opened to trade it could provide a substantial increase in demand for exports, thereby stimulating a revival of business activity in Britain. Doctrinaire free-trade arguments supplemented and supported economic self-interest: a widening of the world's free-trade area would provide an antidote for the slump in the British economy. It was largely on these grounds that influential sections of the commercial public became advocates of the annexation of Upper Burma in 1885–6.

It was Africa, and not Asia that bore the brunt of the new commercial imperialism in the 1880s. The belief that 'over-production' was at the root of the business recession led to considerable mercantile interest in Africa as a possible new market for British manufactures. The only requirment for the success of British trade in Africa, businessmen believed, was the preservation of free trade. At first it was hoped that free trade in Africa might be protected by international guarantees providing equal access for the traders of all nations. Although many British businessmen were suspicious of the 'international' approach of King Leopold of the Belgians, there was a general feeling in business circles that the commercial penetration of Africa could be accomplished without the direct involvement of any European governments. Like the opening of markets in the Far East, it was believed that the economic development of Africa could proceed through private enterprise and international co-operation. This was in fact the general attitude of businessmen at the time of the Berlin West Africa Conference in 1884–5, but such hopes were soon destined to fade. Indeed, at the Berlin Conference itself free trade came under attack from France and Portugal. Moreover, by the mid 1880s free trade no longer corresponded to the realities of European commerce in many parts of

Africa. With the Royal Niger Company and the Congo Free State both intent on building monopolistic systems in their respective spheres on the Niger and the Congo, and with mutual tariff discrimination among British, French and German possessions on the west coast of Africa, free trade was turning out to be a delusion.

By the mid 1880s the Liverpool and Manchester Chambers of Commerce were beginning to advocate not only the partition of parts of the West African coastline then occupied by European powers but also the extension of British influence to 'unoccupied' parts of the coast and even parts of the West African hinterland. Around the same time, powerful groups of businessmen in London and Manchester pressed the British Government to reserve a sphere of influence for Britain in East Africa. Although the reluctance of the British Government and the revival of business activity in Britain after 1886 mitigated the force of this commercial imperialism, it was a decisive factor in shaping the partition of the African continent in the mid 1880s.

Business confidence in Britain recovered to some extent with an improvement in the economic picture after 1886, although international competition for markets raged more fiercely than ever as more and more European countries turned towards protection. Moreover, Manchester became increasingly concerned over Indian competition, which was beginning seriously to affect cotton exports to the Far East. About the same time British merchants in West Africa began to call for official action to break down indigenous barriers to the extension of markets and to protect their trade against French protectionism. They were able to secure support from commercial opinion in Britain because of widespread fears that British exports might be shut out of potentially valuable markets by hostile foreign tariffs. The areas of concern to businessmen in the late 1880s were almost exclusively those where foreign rivalry threatened to destroy existing trade or cut off supposedly rich markets, as in West Africa. Where this factor was not relevant, as in North or East Africa, or where the danger was not yet acute, as in China, commercial opinion in Britain was not particularly concerned. Moreover, it was in those specific areas of West Africa where mercantile opinion in Britain supported the demands of African merchants for intervention, the Gold Coast and Lagos, that the British Government agreed to extensions of British influence.

Commercial pressures for government intervention to preserve free trade abroad increased sharply with the onset of another severe recession in the early 1890s, the proclamation of the Méline tariff and the establishment of the principle of tariff assimilation in the French colonies. The failure of plans for commercial union of the mother country and the settlement colonies and Manchester's continued anxiety over the condition of the Indian market further emphasised the need for the creation of new overseas outlets. Businessmen pressed the government to extend British influence into the hinterlands of tropical Africa to preserve free trade in areas where it was threatened by European protectionism, to break down obstacles set up by indigenous authorities to the free movement of goods through their territories and to impose direct imperial control, as opposed to chartered company rule, in areas where the latter appeared unable or unwilling to provide the framework of security and free trade required for the development of new markets. This interventionism was seen by businessmen as a kind of anti-cyclical policy that would pull the economy out of recession by creating increased demand for British exports.

The course of the partition of Africa in the early 1890s was strongly influenced by these commercial pressures in Britain. In West Africa the extension of British rule in the Gold Coast and the areas that later became Nigeria followed strong mercantile pressures for intervention. In East Africa, mercantile pressure in the metropolis was an important factor in the retention of Uganda. Where commercial pressures were weak, imperial expansion occurred only on a minor scale, as in the Gambia and Sierra Leone. Where there was a strong economic countercurrent, as in southern Africa, metropolitan commercial imperialism was unable to make significant gains. All in all there was a most striking congruence between commercial pressure and imperial expansion in the years from 1870 to 1895.

The appointment of Joseph Chamberlain to the Colonial Office in September 1895 was in some ways the culmination of the commercial imperialism of the 1880s and 1890s. Chamberlain's intention to develop the 'neglected estates' of the tropical empire was simply the official recognition of what the commercial community had been demanding for the previous decade. His appointment to the Colonial Office was enthusiastically applauded by the Press and prominent business leaders. There was widespread approval in business circles for the new Colonial Secretary's proposals to turn the tropical dependencies into adjuncts of the British economy, supplying the mother country with food and raw materials and providing ever-growing markets for the output of British industry. Chamberlain would use the state to pave the way for British enterprise in the tropics. Where it appeared that there were valuable gains to be made, colonial boundaries would be expanded. The British Government would provide the framework of 'law and order' and build railways and other infrastructure required for economic development. This was the height of the imperialism of free trade; the country's economic problems would be solved not by restriction at home, but by imperial expansion and economic development abroad.

Chamberlain's plans for the tropical colonies and dependencies had far-reaching social and economic implications. The Colonial Secretary believed that the development of the vast potential of the tropics would be the salvation of Britain's free trade economic system. Only by expanding overseas markets could the persistent problems of 'over-production' and foreign tariffs be overcome. Without a healthy overseas trade, the domestic economy would collapse, unemployment would increase to dangerous levels and there would be unbearable tensions in the already strained class relations of British society. Like many other European leaders of his day, Chamberlain had a profound fear of social revolution. If the fluctuations in the economy were not modified by conscious government policies to combat economic recession, Chamberlain feared a possible breakdown in the economic system, bringing in its train class warfare and social chaos. The way to avoid these dangers, he believed, was to make the country prosperous by a far-seeing policy of colonial expansion and development.

The influential business classes seemed to demand such a policy in 1895. Indeed the remainder of the decade saw some of the most dramatic episodes in the whole imperialist saga, from the scramble in West Africa to the tumultuous conflict with the Boers in South Africa. Yet little came of Chamberlain's ambition to turn the colonial territories in Africa and Asia into satellites of the British economy. Most of the tropical dependencies remained economic backwaters, stagnating on the periphery of the modern world economy until after the Second World War. Despite the strong commercial pressures for intervention in Africa and Asia in the

1880s and early 1890s, few businessmen were prepared seriously to commit themselves to tropical enterprises. The 'highway to China' was never built as a commercial route—the Burma road was a military project of the twentieth century. So far as Africa was concerned, the whole exercise of the partition had a certain degree of unreality about it: lines drawn on maps did not become actual boundaries until many years later and the tropical markets that businessmen hoped to develop failed to materialise until the mid twentieth century.

Why, after having partitioned much of Africa and Asia in a feverish burst of imperialist activity in the 1880s and 1890s, did Britain and the other European powers then proceed virtually to ignore their tropical possessions until well into the twentieth century? Diverse explanations have been given by historians for this apparent lack of consistency. Moral revulsion against imperialism after the Boer War, the shifting of Great Power rivalries from overseas back to the main European arena in the decade before 1914 are two of the reasons given for Europeans' neglect of the tropics after the period of partition. Some might perhaps suggest that with most of the non-European world already partitioned by the end of the nineteenth century, imperialism had to end. But this would be wrong to equate imperialism with partition. It has been one of the main contentions of this study that partition was simply one stage in the process of imperialism. In the case of the British, partition was a means to an end, the exploitation of the tropics in the interests of the metropolitan economy. There was of course economic exploitation of the tropics long before the 1870s but the wholesale integration of tropical dependencies in Africa and Asia into the European industrialised economies did not occur until the 1930s. This might seem surprising, since it was the avowed intention of the commercial classes to develop new tropical markets for a decade before 1895. In that year they had a Colonial Secretary (Chamberlain) who was determined to use state power to turn the tropics into appendages of the British economy.

There were, certainly, social and political obstacles to the success of Chamberlain's plans for colonial development. Even though they virtually controlled the country's foreign and domestic policies, Victorian middle-class businessmen did not themselves form governments in the late nineteenth century. Most late Victorian administrations were still made up of members of the titled aristocracy. Chamberlain, the Birmingham screw manufacturer who had methodically worked his way up to the highest pinnacles of the political system, was never entirely at home in the cosy complacency of the Victorian country house. Chamberlain was one of the *nouveaux riches*, something it was possible to forgive but not easy to forget in late Victorian society. Yet it was not really this which stood in the way of the success of his colonial policies. By the end of the nineteenth century, the centre of gravity of the social pyramid had shifted to the point where much of the country's wealth and the political power that went with it belonged to men of Chamberlain's class. For the prosperous middle classes in Victorian society social mobility was not so much a matter of being accepted into the aristocracy as of taking over for themselves the trappings of aristocratic society (Chamberlain, for example, sent his sons to Rugby). It was certainly not any lack of social influence or political power that accounted for the business community's failure to exploit the economic potential of the territories that had just been partitioned.

The chief reason for the neglect of the tropical dependencies after partition was not so much political or social as economic. The 1880s and early 1890s were years of economic panic. The appearance of foreign competition in areas of the world where Britain had hitherto enjoyed a virtual monopoly, the recurrent economic recessions and the severe squeeze on profits in the closing decades of the nineteenth century produced a feeling of deep anxiety in the business community. Whether the years from 1873 to 1896 constituted a distinct economic period, a 'Great Depression', is a moot point. Whatever the objective performance of the British economy in this period, and it is hard to deny that there was a slowing down in the rate of growth and serious problems in British industry, there can be no doubt that businessmen believed the country to be suffering from a 'Great Depression'. Convinced that 'over-production' was at the root of the trouble, they desperately sought to open up new markets in Africa and Asia, a process in which they demanded and received the active assistance of the British Government. With the other industrialised countries of Europe pursuing similar objectives at the same time, the upshot was the annexation and partition of large parts of Africa and Asia.

After 1895 the climate of business opinion changed. The recovery of confidence was partly the result of a general improvement in the economic picture, following an upswing in business activity in the second half of the 1890s. There is still vigorous debate among economic historians as to the precise movement of key economic variables during the decades before and after 1895. There is, however, little doubt that by the end of the century businessmen felt that they had left a time of troubles behind them. There was of course the continuing problem of the trade cycle. Profits, for example, recovered after 1895 but fell again in the years following 1901. International competition for markets continued unabated into the twentieth century. But neither cyclical recession nor foreign competition produced the same anxiety in men's minds. Where they had once been regarded as grave threats to the survival of the economic system, slumps and cut-throat international competition came to be accepted as the inevitable concomitants of the system. After about the middle of the 1890s, the crisis appeared to be over. 'All's well that ends well' might have been the conclusion drawn by some contemporaries. It took another generation and an even greater economic crisis before men began to realise that all was not well.

Select bibliography

Primary Sources

A Official Correspondence

1 FOREIGN OFFICE CORRESPONDENCE, Public Record Office, London
Great Britain and General. Under 'Africa', FO 83/1237–44, 1309–1319, 1374–87. Some useful material on a wide range of subjects from diplomatic documents to domestic affairs in Britain, but not yielding a large amount of information relevant to this study.
Slave Trade. Under 'Domestic Various', 1870–92, FO 84/1333, 1335, 1350–1, 1365–6, 1384, 1407, 1425, 1463, 1498–9, 1527, 1556–7, 1585–7, 1611–12, 1630–1, 1654–5, 1681–93, 1731–45, 1779–96, 1856–74, 1914–35, 1986–2009, 2027–98, 2154–81, 2239–2266; 'Correspondence Relating to the Congo', 1882–4, FO 84/1802–10; 'Correspondence Relating to the Berlin West African Conference', 1884–5, FO 84/1812–23. 'Resolutions from Chambers of Commerce on Uganda', FO 84/2192. The Slave Trade series contains original correspondence, including official Minutes, on African affairs. The 'Domestic Various' category has valuable material on Africa from a variety of sources, including individual businessmen and business groups.

2 COLONIAL OFFICE CORRESPONDENCE, Public Record Office, London
Correspondence Relating to the Gambia, 1870–95, CO 87/98A, 101, 103, 106, 108, 109, 110, 114, 117, 119, 121, 125–50.

Correspondence Relating to the Gold Coast, 1870–95, CO 96/86, 91, 108–10, 114, 117, 119, 134, 136, 144, 146–7, 150, 154, 155, 158, 163, 166–7, 170–1, 173, 175–6, 179, 183, 185–93, 198–200, 202, 205, 207–10, 212, 214–15, 217–21, 228–9, 232, 239–40, 242–4, 246–50, 254–63.
Correspondence Relating to Lagos, 1870–9, 1888–95, CO 147/22, 25, 26, 29, 31, 32, 64, 70–3, 74–6, 79–97, 100, 102–3.
Correspondence Relating to Sierra Leone, 1870–95, CO 267/324, 325, 345, 347, 348–9, 354–8, 360–6, 368–70, 373–7, 379, 381–5, 387–9, 392–423.

3 FOREIGN OFFICE CONFIDENTIAL PRINT
The Foreign Office and Colonial Office Confidential Print are collections of printed papers containing selected correspondence, memoranda and other documents intended for cabinet circulation. Minutes are usually not included. These papers present material from a wide variety of official documents which is focused on a particular issue or problem.
FO 403/14, 15A, 15B, 36–9: Correspondence on the Anglo-Portuguese Congo Treaty.
FO 403/46–50: Correspondence on the Berlin West Africa Conference.

4 COLONIAL OFFICE CONFIDENTIAL PRINT
CO 879/7/75. West Africa, 1874–5. Proposed exchange of possessions with France.
CO 879/8/77. West Africa, 1875–7. Exchange of possessions with France. Further correspondence.
CO 879/9/92. West Africa, 1875–6. Affairs and proposed exchange of possessions with France.
CO 879/25/333. West Africa, 1886–8. Affairs. Further correspondence.
CO 879/27/345. West Africa, 1887–8. Territorial questions and proposed negotiations with France. Further correspondence.
CO 879/28/355. West Africa, 1888. Territorial questions with France in the neighbourhood of Lagos, and proposed negotiations on various West African matters. Further correspondence.
CO 879/38/448. Gold Coast, 1892–4. Mission of Mr Ferguson into interior. Correspondence.

B Private Papers

1 MINUTES OF CHAMBERS OF COMMERCE

These vary immensely in the amount of material they yield. The Records of the Manchester Chamber are fairly complete, though they still need to be supplemented by newspaper reports. The Liverpool Chamber's Records are fragmentary and of little value; information on its proceedings had to be obtained from Liverpool newspapers. Records of the Chambers of Glasgow, Birmingham and London provided sufficient material for the purposes of this study when used in conjunction with the Chambers' printed Annual Reports.

Minutes of the Council of the Birmingham Chamber of Commerce, 1870–95 (in the Offices of the Birmingham Chamber of Commerce).

Minutes of the Board of Directors of the Glasgow Chamber of Commerce, 1870–95 (in the Offices of the Glasgow Chamber of Commerce).

Minutes of the Council of the Liverpool Chamber of Commerce, 1883–95. Minutes of the East India and China Committee of the Liverpool Chamber of Commerce, 1891–5 (in the City of Liverpool Public Library).

Minutes of the Council of the London Chamber of Commerce, 1888–95. Minutes of the West African Section of the London Chamber of Commerce, 1884–95. Minutes of the South African Section of the London Chamber of Commerce, 1884–95 (in the Offices of the London Chamber of Commerce).

Proceedings of the Manchester Chamber of Commerce, 1870–1895.

Minutes of the African Sectional Committee of the Manchester Chamber of Commerce, 1892–5 (in the City of Manchester Public Library).

2 BUSINESSMEN'S PAPERS

A variety of these was consulted, though in most cases the yield of material for the purposes of this study was extremely low. Two particular sources are worth mentioning: the *Mackinnon Papers* at the School of Oriental and African Studies, University of London, and the *John Holt Papers*, in the possession of the John Holt Company, Liverpool, provided some useful material.

C Published Documentary Sources

1 CHAMBER OF COMMERCE REPORTS

Annual Reports of the Birmingham Chamber of Commerce, 1870–1895.
Annual Reports of the Glasgow Chamber of Commerce, 1870–95.
Annual Reports of the Liverpool Chamber of Commerce, 1870–95.
Annual Reports of the London Chamber of Commerce, 1882–95.
Annual Reports of the Manchester Chamber of Commerce, 1870–1895.
Reports of the Association of Chambers of Commerce of the United Kingdom, 1870–95.
Reports of the Proceedings of the Congress of Chambers of Commerce of the Empire, 1886, 1892.
Annual Reports of the African Trade Section of the Liverpool Chamber of Commerce.

2 BRITISH PARLIAMENTARY PAPERS

Particularly useful was the First Report of the Royal Commission appointed to inquire into the Depression of Trade and Industry; 1886 (C. 4621) XXI. Second Report, with Evidence and Appendix, Pt. II, 1886 (C. 4715) XXI, 231. Appendix, Pt. I, 1886 (4715–1) XXII. Third Report, with Evidence and Appendix, 1886 (C. 4797) XXIII, 1. Final Report, with Evidence and Appendix, 1886 (C. 4893) XXIII, 507.

D Newspapers and periodicals

Several of these were essential in providing information on the state of commercial opinion, particularly in Lancashire, and supplementing records of chambers of commerce.

Chamber of Commerce Journal, 1882–95.
The Economist, 1880–95.
Liverpool Daily Courier, 1870–95.
Liverpool Journal of Commerce, 1870–95.
Manchester Guardian, 1870–95.

Secondary Sources

A large number of specialised works was consulted in the preparation of this study. Those listed below were used in the text or cited in the references.

A Books

AJAYI, J. F. ADE, and SMITH, ROBERT E., *Yoruba Warfare in the Nineteenth Century*, Cambridge, 1964.

ALDCROFT, D. H. (ed.), *The Development of British Industry and Foreign Competition 1875–1914*, London, 1968.

ALLEN, G. C., *The Industrial Development of Birmingham and the Black Country 1860–1927*, New York, 1966 ed.

ASHLEY, P., *Modern Tariff History*, London, 1920.

AUNG, MAUNG HTIN, *The Stricken Peacock: Anglo-Burmese Relations 1752–1948*, The Hague, 1965.

AYDELOTTE, W. O., *Bismarck and British Colonial Policy*, Philadelphia, 1937.

BODELSEN, C. A., *Studies in Mid-Victorian Imperialism*, Copenhagen, 1924.

BROWN, BENJAMIN H., *The Tariff Reform Movement in Great Britain 1881–95*, New York, 1943.

CADY, JOHN F., *A History of Modern Burma*, New York, 1958.

CLOUGH, S. B., *France. A History of National Economics 1789–1939*, New York, 1939.

COLQUHOUN, A. R., and HALLETT, H., *Report on the Railway Connection of Burma and China*, London, 1888.

COUPLAND, R., *The Exploitation of East Africa 1856–1890*, London, 1939.

CROWE, S. E., *The Berlin West African Conference, 1884–85*, New York, 1942.

DAVENPORT, T. R. H., *The Afrikaner Bond. The History of a South African Political Party*, Cape Town, 1966.

EASTMAN, LLOYD, *Throne and Mandarins. China's Search for a Policy during the Sino-French Controversy 1880–85*, Cambridge, Mass., 1967.

ELDRIDGE, C. C., *England's Mission: The Imperial Idea in the Age of Gladstone and Disraeli 1868–1880*, London, 1973.

ELLISON, T., *The Cotton Trade in Great Britain*, London, 1886.

FLINT, JOHN E., *Sir George Goldie and the Making of Nigeria*, London, 1960.

FYFE, CHRISTOPHER, *A History of Sierra Leone*, Oxford, 1962.

GAILEY, H. A., *A History of the Gambia*, New York, 1965.

GALBRAITH, JOHN S., *Mackinnon and East Africa 1878–95. A Study in the New Imperialism*, Cambridge, 1972.

GALLAGHER, JOHN, and ROBINSON, RONALD, *Africa and the Victorians. The Official Mind of Imperialism*, London, 1961.

GIBSON, MARTIN, W. A., *A Century of Liverpool's Commerce, 1850–1950*, Liverpool, 1950.

GIFFORD, PROSSER, and LOUIS, W. R. (eds), *Britain and Germany in Africa. Imperial Rivalry and Colonial Rule*, London, 1967.

GIRAULT, ARTHUR, *The Colonial Tariff Policy of France*, London, 1916.

HALL, D. G. E., *A History of South-East Asia*, London, 1964.

HARGREAVES, J. D., *Prelude to the Partition of West Africa*, London, 1963.

HARNETTY, PETER, *Imperialism and Free Trade: Lancashire and India in the Mid-Nineteenth Century*, Vancouver, 1972.

HELM, E., *A History of the Manchester Chamber of Commerce*, London, 1902.

HERTSLET, E., *Map of Africa by Treaty*, London, 1896.

HOFFMAN, WALTHER G., *British Industry, 1700–1950*, New York, 1965.

HOPKINS A. G., *An Economic History of West Africa*, London, 1973.

HSÜ, IMMANUEL C. Y., *The Rise of Modern China*, New York, 1970.

HYDE, F. E., *Liverpool and the Mersey: An Economic History of a Port*, Liverpool, 1971.

IKIME, OBARO, *Merchant Prince of the Niger Delta*, London, 1968.

ILERSIC, A. R., and LIDDLE, P. F. B., *Parliament of Commerce: The Story of the Association of British Chambers of Commerce 1860–1960*, London, 1960.

KANYA-FORSTNER, A. S., *The Conquest of the Western Sudan. A Study in French Military Imperialism*, Cambridge, 1969.

KENDLE, JOHN, *The Colonial and Imperial Conferences 1887–1911*, London, 1967.

KIERNAN, E. V. G., *British Diplomacy in China 1880–85*, New York, 1970.

KIMBLE, DAVID, *A Political History of Ghana*, Oxford, 1963.

148

KOEBNER, R., *Imperialism: The Story and Significance of a Political Word*, Cambridge, 1964.

MCPHEE, ALLAN, *The Economic Revolution in British West Africa*, London, 1926.

MAN, E. GARNET, *The Present Trade Crisis Critically Examined*, London, 1885.

MITCHELL, B. R., and DEANE, P., *Abstract of British Historical Statistics*, London, 1962.

MUSGRAVE, C. E., *The London Chamber of Commerce, 1881–1914*, London, 1914.

NEWBURY, C. W., *The Western Slave Coast and its Rulers: European Trade and Administration among the Yoruba and Adja-Speaking Peoples of Southwestern Nigeria, Southern Dahomey and Togo*, Oxford, 1961.

OLIVER, R., *The Missionary Factor in East Africa*, London, 1952.

—*Sir Harry Johnston and the Scramble for Africa*, London, 1957.

PELCOVITS, NATHAN, A., *Old China Hands and the Foreign Office*, New York, 1948.

PLATT, D. C. M., *Finance, Trade and Politics in British Foreign Policy 1815–1914*, Oxford, 1968.

REDFORD, ARTHUR, *Manchester Merchants and Foreign Trade, II: 1850–1939*, New York, 1967.

SAUL, S. B., *Studies in British Overseas Trade, 1870–1914*, Liverpool, 1960.

SCHLOTE, W. *British Overseas Trade*, Oxford, 1952.

SCHUYLER, R. L., *The Fall of the Old Colonial System. A Study in British Free Trade, 1770–1870*, London, 1945.

SILLERY, ANTHONY, *John Mackenzie of Bechuanaland 1835–1899*, Cape Town, 1971.

SINGHAL, D. P., *The Annexation of Upper Burma*, Singapore, 1960.

TAYLOR, A. J. P., *Germany's First Bid for Colonies*, London, 1938.

THORP, W. L., *Business Annals*, New York, 1926.

TOWNSEND, M. E., *Origins of Modern German Colonialism*, New York, 1921.

TYLER, J. E., *The Struggle for Imperial Unity 1868–1895*, London, 1938.

WANG, S. T., *The Margary Affair and the Chefoo Agreement*, Oxford, 1940.

WOODHOUSE, C. M., and LOCKHART, J. C., *Rhodes*, London, 1963.

WOODMAN, DOROTHY, *The Making of Burma*, London, 1962.

WRIGHT, G. H., *Chronicles of the Birmingham Chamber of Commerce*, Birmingham, 1913.
WRIGHT, MARY C., *The Last Stand of Chinese Conservatism. The T'ung Chih Restoration, 1862 to 1874*, Stanford, California, 1957.

B Articles

CHECKLAND, S. G., 'The Mind of the City, 1870–1914', *Oxford Economic Papers*, Oct. 1957, pp. 261–78.
DACHS, ANTHONY, 'Missionary Imperialism—the Case of Bechuanaland', *Journal of African History*, xiii, 1972, pp. 633–54.
GALBRAITH, J. S., 'Myths of the Little England Era', *American Historical Review*, 67, Oct. 1961, pp. 34–48.
HARNETTY, PETER, 'The Indian Cotton Duties Controversy, 1894–96', *English Historical Review*, 2nd ser., lxxvii, Oct. 1962, pp. 684–702.
HOPKINS, A. G., 'Economic Imperialism in West Africa: Lagos 1880–92', *Economic History Review*, 2nd ser., xxi, 1968, pp. 580–606.
MACDONAGH, OLIVER, 'The Anti-Imperialism of Free Trade', *Economic History Review*, 2nd ser., xiv, 1961, pp. 489–501.
MCINTYRE, W. D., 'Commander Glover and the Colony of Lagos, 1861–1873', *Journal of African History*, iv, 1963, pp. 57–79.
MCLEAN, DAVID, 'Commerce, Finance, and British Diplomatic Support in China, 1885–86', *Economic History Review*, 2nd ser., xxvi, 1973, pp. 464–76.
NEWBURY, C. W., 'The Protectionist Revival in French Colonial Trade: The Case of Senegal', *Economic History Review*, 2nd ser., xxi, 1968, pp. 331–48.
PLATT, D. C. M., 'The Imperialism of Free Trade: Some Reservations', *Economic History Review*, 2nd ser., xxi, 1968, pp. 296–306.
— 'Further Objections to an "Imperialism of Free Trade", 1830–60', *Economic History Review*, 2nd ser., xxvi, 1973, pp. 77–91.

C Theses

DAVIES, P. N., 'Sir Alfred Lewis Jones and the Development of West African Trade'. University of Liverpool, M.A. thesis, 1963.
DUMMETT, R. E., 'British Official Attitudes in Relation to Economic

Development in the Gold Coast, 1874–1905'. University of London, Ph.D. thesis, 1966.

GERTZEL, C., 'John Holt: A British Merchant in West Africa in the Era of Imperialism'. Oxford University, Ph.D. thesis, 1959.

THOMPSON, WILLIAM, 'Glasgow and Africa: Connections and Attitudes, 1870–1900'. University of Strathclyde, Ph.D. thesis, 1970.

South east Asia

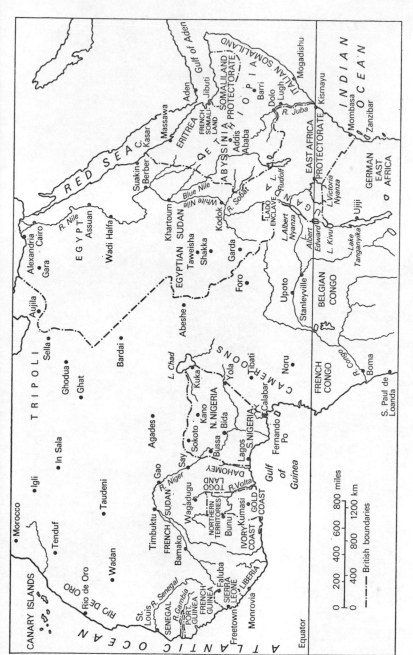

Tropical Africa (east and west)

Southern Africa

Mombasa
Zanzibar
Lindi
Mozambique
GERMAN EAST AFRICA
R. Rovuma
Lake Nyasa
Ujiji
Lake Tanganyika
Kilimane
EAST AFRICA
NYASALAND PROT.
Sofola
PORTUGUESE
Lake Bangweolo
Inhambane
Lorenco Marques
Kazembe
R. Zambezi
BELGIAN CONGO
Sitanda
Salisbury
Lialui
RHODESIA
Victoria Falls
Bulawayo
Durban
Ndaro
Moremi
R. Limpopo
Pretoria
TRANSVAAL
NATAL
R. Congo
Boma
ANGOLA
ORANGE R. COLONY
Bloemfontein
Kuruman
Orange R.
S. Paul de Loanda
GERMAN SOUTH WEST AFRICA
Warmbad
Port Elizabeth
Benguela
Bethany
Port Nolloth
CAPE COLONY
Walfish Bay
Cape Town
MADAGASCAR

| 0 | 200 | 400 | 600 | 800 miles |
| 0 | 400 | 800 | 1200 km |

-·-·- British boundaries

Index

Abeokuta, 98;
  Treaty of, 99, 100
Admiralty, 82
adulteration of goods, 94
Africa, East, 19, 20, 29, 77–83, 128–129, 137;
  (and see Anglo-German Partition Agreement)
Africa, West, 18, 19, 29, 37, 63, 96–97, 118–19, 120–1, 137;
  (and see Cotton; Free Trade)
Africa and the Victorians: The Official Mind of Imperialism, 5, 6
African Association, 62, 101, 102, 124
African Committee (see Manchester Chamber of Commerce)
African Exploration Fund, 24
Algeria, 111, 120
Amatongaland, 104
Anderson, Percy, 70, 77, 81
Andrew, S., 46
Anglo-Chinese relations, 16, 28–9
  (and see China)
Anglo-French Commercial Treaty (see Cobden Treaty); (1882), 35
Anglo-French Convention (1889), 96, 100–1, 116, 118, 119, 121, 122
  (and see France; Sierra Leone)
Anglo-German partition agreement (E. Africa), 81–2, 103, 116, 127, 137, 138, 140
  (and see Germany; Bismarck)
Anglo-Portuguese Treaty, 60, 61, 62, 64, 65; abandoned (1884), 66, 101;
  (and see Portugal)
Anglo-Spanish relations, 34;
  (and see Spain)
Annam, 50
Arakan, 50
Arms trade, 23, 41, 42, 61, 63
Arts, Society of, 31
Ashanti, 76, 96, 97, 121–2
Ashworth (President of Manchester Chamber of Commerce), 34
Assam, 50
Association of UK Chamber of Commerce, 14, 15, 35, 46–7, 67, 91, 113

Basutoland, 104
Bechuanaland, 104
Belgium, 58, 59, 66;
  arms exports, 41, 63
Benin, Bight of, 76
Benue River, 75, 76, 124
Berlin, 70
Berlin West Africa Conference (1884–5), 68, 69, 70, 71, 72, 76, 136
Biafra, 76
Birmingham:
  Chamber of Commerce, 14, 23–4, 41, 61;
    opposition to Congo Treaty, 63; Annual Report (1891), 109; and W. African trade,

120–1; and Swaziland railway, 127; and Uganda, 128; metallurgical trades, 23; small arms trade, 23, 41, 42, 61; protectionism, 36, 42 (*and see* protectionism); recession of 1884, 63; and Imperial preference, 90, 113

Bismarck, Chancellor, 66, 68, 73, 76, 78, 80; *Schutzbrief*, 78

Blackburn, 31

Boers, 105, 127, 139, 140

Bombay (textile mills), 27

Bradford, 60

Bradshaw, James, 29–30, 31

Brass (city), 126

brass-working trades, 23

Brazza, Savorgnan de, 58, 59

Bright, Jacob, MP, 60, 62, 65, 72, 79

Britain: economic growth, 7, 8, 35, 135, 141–2

gross domestic product (GDP), 13, 22, 35, 109; business attitudes to colonies, 8, 9, 14; recessions (1873–9), 22ff., 27, 88, 134; (1883–6), 40, 43, 57, 62, 88, 109, 135, 141; (1890s), 90, 115, 119, 141; Joint Commission on E. Africa, 81; booms (1886), 88, 137; (late 1890s), 142; class structure, 139, 141; (*and see* all Anglo-entries)

British East Africa Association, 79

British East Africa Company, 128

British South Africa Company, 105

Broadhurst, Henry, 79

Buganda, 127

Burma: trade with, 17, 50–2

railway projects in, 37, 49–50, 92, 110, 115, 136, 140; wars with Britain, 50; British occupation (1886), 52, 54, 92

button trade (Birmingham), 23

Cameroons, 68

Canada: tariffs (1860), 14;

protectionism, 27, 36, 47; and Imperial Preference, 109, 113

Cape Colony, 103, 104, 127

Cape Dutch Party, 105

Cape route, security of, 6

Carter, Governor G. T., 123

Catholicism, 58

Chamberlain, Joseph, 104, 122, 126, 138, 139, 140, 141

Chambers of Commerce of the Empire:

1886 Congress, 48; 1892 Congress, 112–14

Chambers of Commerce, UK Association (*see* Association) (*and see* Glasgow, Liverpool, London and Manchester)

China: trade with, 16, 17, 28, 45, 48, 54, 110, 115, 135–6, 137; famine, 24; relations with Britain (*see* Anglo-Chinese); railway projects into, 37, 92, 115; relations with France (*see* France)

China Association, 115

Chefoo Convention (1876), 29

Churchill, Lord Randolph, 50

Church Missionary Society, 127

Cobden Treaty, 13, 14, 26

Cochin China, 50

Coke, H., 99

Colonial and Indian Exhibition, 90

Colonial Office, 37, 74, 96, 97, 98, 100, 102, 105, 118, 120, 121, 123, 138

Colquhoun, A. R., 46, 48, 49, 50

Columbus, Christopher, 1

Commerce, Chambers of (*see* Chambers of Commerce)

Congo District Defence Association, 64

Congo Free State, 137

Congo River basin, 57–8, 71; trade with, 61, 62, 66, 71; import duties, 69, 70; boundaries, 72

(*and see* Anglo-Portuguese Treaty; Leopold)

Cooper, T. T., 17
Cotton: production, 4, 45, 109;
  importance to British economy,
  10; 'famine' of 1860s, 15;
  recessions: late 1870s, 24–5, 29,
  33;
    1880s, 44, 70, 75, 88; 1892,
    114;
  exports, 79, 89;
    to India, 22, 27, 36, 37; slump
    in, 25, 110, 137; to Italy, 89;
    to W. Africa, 125–6;
    (and see India; Lancashire;
    Manchester; USA)
Cotton Spinners and Manu-
  facturers' Association of N. and
  N.E. Lancs., 46
Cranborne, Lord, 17
customs duties, 28, 69, 70
  (and see India; Protectionism)
Customs Union projects, 126

Denton, Acting-Governor G. C.,
  123
Depression, Great, 8, 11, 141
  (and see Britain)
Dick, Walter D., 51
Dilke, Sir C. W., 59
Dunn, William, 105

Economist, The, 45
economy (see Britain)
edge tools trade (Birmingham), 23
Edwards Bros. & Co., 95
Egba tribe, 123–4
Egypt, 82
Elder Dempster Lines, 125
emigration policy, 26, 47, 53, 79
Employers' Association of N. and
  N.E. Lancs., 44
Enfield Co., 41
  (and see arms trade)
exports, 3, 35, 40, 109
  (and see Britain; Cotton)

Factory legislation, 91
famines, 24
Ferguson, George, 121

Findlay, James, and Co., 51
Fitzmaurice, Lord, 78
Foot, Captain, 32
Foreign Office, 26, 58, 59, 60, 61,
  62, 64, 65, 67, 68, 70, 71, 72, 74,
  77, 79, 80, 81, 97, 98, 100, 103,
  117, 118, 124, 127, 128
Foster, W. E., MP, 60
France, 13, 14, 35, 36, 73, 120;
  colonies, 14, 138; Gambia
  negotiations with Britain, 19;
  protectionism, 26, 35, 36, 45, 67,
  69, 103, 110, 111, 136–7;
  relations with China, 49;
  expansion into S.E. Asia, 50–1,
  89, 115; and the Congo, 59, 66,
  67, 71; expansion into Africa, 89,
  97–8, 100–1; tariff assimilation
  policy, 111, 112, 138; and Sierra
  Leone, 120
  (and see Abeokuta; Anglo-French
  and Franco- entries)
Franco-Chinese Treaty (1885), 49
Franco-Prussian War, 19, 24, 41
Franco-Siamese Treaty (1893),
  115, 116
Freetown, 117
free trade, 13, 25, 26, 40, 41, 50, 52,
  69, 91;
  pros and cons of, 42, 46, 93, 134,
  135, 139; with Africa, 57, 61, 73,
  81, 103, 129; and Portuguese
  Treaty, 64, 66, 67; and Niger
  Company, 129; annexation of
  Upper Burma, 136
Free Trade Hall (Manchester), 65
Froude, James A., 89

Gallagher, John, 5, 6
Galloway, John, 51, 52
Gambia, the, 19, 75, 95, 96, 101,
  138
Germany, 66, 73, 103
  colonial expansion, 68, 69, 74, 76,
  77, 78, 80; and Joint Commission
  with Britain, 81, 82
  (and see Bismarck)
Ghana, 121

Gladstone, Robert S., 54
Gladstone, S. S., 53
Gladstone, W. E., 58, 68, 78
Glasgow Chamber of Commerce,
    42, 49, 50, 51, 52, 59, 103, 110,
    117, 121, 122;
    opposition to Congo Treaty, 63;
    and Niger Company, 125; and
    Swaziland railway project, 127;
    and Uganda, 128
Glover, John, 18, 19
Gold Coast, 37, 74–6, 95, 96, 97,
    101, 102, 116, 122, 137, 138
Goldie, George, 71, 76, 77, 124, 125
Gold Standard, 135
Grafton, F. W., 31, 32
Granville, George Granville
    Leveson-Gower, 2nd Earl, 72,
    78, 79, 80
Griffith, Bradford, 122
groundnuts (India), 93
Guinea, Gulf of, 68, 74
guns (see Arms trade)

Hamburg, 69
Hay, Sir John, 95
Heligoland Treaty, 103
Helm, E., 72
Hill, Clement, 78
Hobson, J. A., 4
Hofmeyr, Jan, 105
Holmwood, Frederick, 32, 33, 77,
    78, 79
Holt, John, and Co., 43, 125
Hong Kong Chamber of Com-
    merce, 49, 115
Houldsworth, William, MP, 72, 79
Hutchinson, George, 99
Hutton, James F., 32, 59, 60, 63,
    70, 71, 72, 79, 80, 81, 82, 126

Ijebu tribe, 123, 124
Imperial Customs Union project,
    90–1
Imperial Federation League (1884),
    89
Imperial Preference, 109, 110, 112,
    113

Imperialism, 1, 5, 6, 44
    classic economic interpretation
    of, 4–5; and security of Cape and
    Suez routes, 6; nineteenth-
    century expansion, 7, 135; and
    inter-Imperial co-operation, 47,
    89; and the partition of Africa,
    140
import duties (see Customs duties)
India, 15, 16, 22, 24, 77;
    and UK cotton trade, 24, 27, 28,
    30, 34, 37, 45, 91, 92, 137, 138;
    import duties, 25, 27, 34, 36, 37,
    91, 114, 115; cotton exports, 77;
    (and see cotton; Lancashire)
India Office, 34, 52
Indo-China, 112, 115, 136
Industrial Revolution, 1, 2, 29, 88
International Association (Congo),
    66, 67, 68, 71, 72, 73, 136
Irish Home Rule, 89
iron and steel trades (see
    Metallurgical trades)
Irrawaddy Flotilla Company, 51
Italy, 89

Jenkins, E., MP, 32
jewellery trades (Birmingham), 23
Johnston, H. H., 77, 81, 82
Jones, A. L., 125
Journal (of London Chamber of
    Commerce), 43–4, 71;
    and China trade, 48; Burma
    trade, 53; Congo, 61–2;
    Imperial preference plan, 112;
    East African markets, 129

Kilimanjaro concession, 77, 78, 79,
    81, 82
Kimberley, John Wodehouse, 1st
    Earl of, 19, 53
Kipini, 82
Kirk, John, 60
Knutsford, Sir Henry Holland, 1st
    Baron, 99, 118
Kumasi, 97, 122

Ladak, 17

Lagos, 3;
  trade with, 18, 74, 95, 96, 98,
  102, 121, 137; French influence,
  97–9, 101, 122; and Yoruba tolls,
  123, 124
Lancashire: and Burma trade, 17–
  18;
W. African trade, 19, 37; slumps
  (1870s), 24–6, 27, 31; (1884), 65,
  77, 109; (1892), 114, 135; and
  Indian exports, 28, 34, 91–2;
  (and see cotton; India)
'law and order', 94, 95, 139
Lee, Henry, MP, 79
Leopold, King of the Belgians, 58,
  60, 61, 66, 67, 68, 73, 136
Liberal Party, 54, 64
Liberia, 66
Lisbon, 64
Lister, T. Villiers, 77
Liverpool:
  Chamber of Commerce, 15, 24,
  37, 117;
    West African Section, 43;
    African Trade Section, 93, 99,
    102, 124, 125;
  trade with Burma, 17, 53–4;
  Lagos, 19, 74; shipping trades,
  24, 88, 125 (and see shipping);
  and Gold Coast railway, 37;
  slump (mid-1880s), 42–3;
  African trade, 42–3, 74, 96, 110,
  120–1, 137; commission houses,
  43; and the Congo, 59, 62; and
  Yorubaland trade, 98, 123–4;
  merchants' criticism of Niger
  Co., 101, 125 (and see Royal
  Niger Company); and Sierra
  Leone, 118–19; Swaziland
  railway, 127; Uganda, 128
Liverpool Mercury, the, 119
London Chamber of Commerce,
  43–4, 48, 89–90, 110;
  and Burma trade, 49–50, 52–3;
  Journal, 43–4, 71; and Lagos, 61;
  West African Trade Section, 63,
  71, 74, 77, 96–7, 100, 125;
  Conference (1886), 90; forces

UK into colonisation, 121;
S. Africa Trade Section, 127
London Merchants, Committee of,
  16
Lugard, Captain F. D., 128

Macfie, R. A., MP, 15
Mackenzie, John, 104
Mackinnon East Africa Company,
  127
Mackinnon, William, 60, 79, 80, 81
Madagascar, 19, 103
Malet, Sir Edward, 72
Man, E. Garnet, 52
Manchester:
  Chamber of Commerce, 15, 26,
  34, 36, 37, 44, 45, 49, 50, 76, 117;
    advocacy of free trade, 46 (and
    see Free Trade); African
    Committee, 65, 72, 73, 79, 82,
    120–1, 126;
  Burma trade, 17, 54 (and see
  Burma); Lagos and Yorubaland
  trade, 19, 123–4; slumps: (late
  1870s), 24–5, 26, 27; (1880s), 44,
  45, 57, 75; (1891), 111, 138;
  campaigns against Indian duties
  (1875–9), 28, 36–7; (1894), 114–
  115; African trade, 31–4, 37, 77,
  95, 96, 120–1, 137; and Congo,
  59–63, 67, 69; and the Niger, 71;
  East African trade, 78–81; and
  Sierra Leone, 118–19; Swaziland
  railway, 127; and Uganda, 129
Manchester Geographical Society,
  34
Manchester Guardian, 70
Mandalay, 51, 52, 53, 92, 115
Manyanga, 73
Matabeleland, 105
Maxwell, Sir William, 122
McKinley tariff, 89
Méline tariff, 111, 119, 138
Mellacourie River, 117, 118
metallurgical trades, 22, 23, 109
  (and see Birmingham)
middlemen system (Africa), 94, 97
Mindon Min, King, 50, 51

missionaries, 104, 127
Moloney, Governor (Sir) Alfred, 100
Mozambique tariff (1877), 62–3
Murray, Kenric B., 43

National African Co., 71, 76, 79
Nigeria, 116, 121, 138
Niger Coast Protectorate (1891), 124, 126
Niger Company (*see* Royal Niger Co.)
Niger Delta Protectorate, 76, 77
Niger River, 71, 72, 75, 76, 101, 124, 125
Nile River, 82
Nokki, 59, 73
Northcote, Sir Stafford, 17

Oceana, 89
Ogowe River, 71
Oil Rivers, 93, 101, 102, 126
Oldham Chamber of Commerce, 69, 70
Oldham Master Cotton Spinners Association, 46
'over-production': of cotton, 25, 26, 44;
general, 41, 42, 135, 141

Pakenham, Thomas Conolly, British Consul in Madagascar, 19
Palmerston, Henry John Temple, 3rd Viscount, 58
palm kernels, 93
palm oil trade, 18–19, 43, 93;
price slump (1886–90), 93
Parkes, J. F., 117
partition (of Africa) (*see* Anglo-German agreement)
Pegu, 50
Peking, 28, 49
Peters, Karl, 78
petroleum resources, 93
Pondoland, 104
Porto Nove, 98, 101
Portugal: Treaty with (1884), 58, 59, 60, 61, 62, 65;

trade with Africa, 59, 69; tariffs, 64, 136; abandoned, 66, 101; and the Congo, 71, 72, 73
Prange, F., 15
Preston (unemployment in), 25, 29–30
Protectionism: Europe, 26–7, 42, 58, 89, 92, 111, 112, 115, 134, 138;
France, 35–6, 45, 49, 92, 103, 137, 138; Canada, 27, 36, 47;
Portugal, 58; Italy, 89; Britain, 110 (*and see* Birmingham); USA, 112, 115
Protectorates, 103, 104
Protestantism, 58

Railways:
E. Africa and Zanzibar, 30, 32, 79, 80, 110;
Burma-China, 37, 48, 49–50, 92, 110, 136; Gold Coast, 76;
Swaziland, 127
Rangoon, 50–2, 136;
Chamber of Commerce, 49, 50
Rawlinson, Joshua, 46
recessions (*see* Britain; Cotton)
Rhodes, Cecil, 104, 105, 116
Ripon, 1st Marquess of, 122
Robinson, Sir Hercules, 105
Robinson, Ronald, 5, 6
Rothschild, Baron P. M. de, 79
Royal Commission on Cotton Industry, 44
Royal Commission on the Depression of Trade and Industry, 46
Royal Geographical Society, 24, 77
Royal Niger Company, 92–3, 101, 124, 125, 126, 128, 137

Saddlery and harness trades (Birmingham), 23
Salford, Bishop of, 32, 33
Salisbury, Robert Cecil, 3rd Marquess of, 54, 65, 80, 110, 118, 121

Samori, King, 117, 118
Seeley, John, 89
Sefwi chiefs, 97
Senegal, 116, 120;
    French Customs duties, 26;
    International Control plan, 71
Shan States, 51, 53
Shaw, R. B., 17
shipping trades, 24, 88, 102, 124;
    ocean rates, 93; W. African
    route, 93, 102; Parliamentary
    lobby, 102
    (*and see* Liverpool)
Siam, 53, 111, 115, 116
Sierra Leone, 75, 76, 95, 101, 117,
    138;
    Anglo-French Commission, 116,
    119; delimitation survey, 117,
    118, 119, 120, 121
Singapore Chamber of Commerce,
    49
Slagg, John, MP, 33, 45, 59, 72, 79,
    80
slave trade, 128
slumps (*see* Britain; cotton)
Society for the Study of Com-
    mercial Geography, 33, 34
South Africa, 103–4
South African Committee, 104
Spain (Tariffs), 26, 34
Sprye, Captain Richard, 17
Stanley, H. M., 59, 67
strikes: (1878), 25; (1883), 44;
    (1884), 45, 69
Suez Canal: security of, 6;
    opening (1869), 27, 93
Swaziland, 104, 105;
    railway project, 127
Sykes, Callander & Co., 95

tallow (Australian), 93
Tanga, 79
tariffs (*see* Protectionism)
Tenasserim, 50
textile trades (*see* Cotton)
The Expansion of England, 89
Thibaw, King, 51, 53, 54
Thomson, Joseph, 77

Tientsin, Treaty of (1858), 16;
    Franco-Chinese Treaty of
    (1885), 49
Togoland, 74
tolls (*see* Yorubaland)
Tonkin, 49, 50, 116, 136
Trade, Board of, 19
trade cycles, 142 (*and see* Britain)
Trades Union Congress, 31
Transkei, 104
Transvaal, 105
Tswana, 104
Tunghi Bay, 82

Uganda, 116, 127, 128;
    British acquisition of, 129, 138
unemployment, 41
    (*and see* Britain; cotton; strikes)
United States: civil war, 4;
    Madagascar trade, 19; wool
    imports from Britain, 22; trade
    with Britain, 23; cotton crop, 44;
    and the Congo, 66; tariffs, 89;
    petroleum resources, 93
Upper Niger (*see* Niger)

Viard, Capitaine, 98, 100
Viard Treaty, 99
Victoria (State of) protectionism,
    47
Victoria Nyanza, Lake, 80

Watson, Sir James, 52
Weavers' Association, 25–6
West African Trade Section (*see*
    London Chamber of Commerce)
West Africa Conference (*see*
    Berlin)
Whitley, E., MP, 62
Witu Treaty, 81
Witwatersrand gold reef, 103
Woermann, Adolf, 69, 73
wool exports, 22, 88, 89

Yorubaland, 18, 98, 122;
    tolls, 123; peace settlement of
    1891, 123–4

Zambesia, 104
Zambezi River, 104
Zanzibar, 32, 77, 80;

railway project, 30, 32–3; Sultan
of, 32–3, 76, 78, 79, 80, 81; and
Germany, 76, 81–2